"People don't take trips—
trips take people."

John Steinbeck, the writer who first inspired
WILDSAM, wrote those words in his American
epic *Travels with Charley*. They capture the core
belief of the book you now hold in your hands:
That unforgettable experiences are born from the
unexpected. And road trips, most especially, beg the
traveler to write plans in pencil and trace routes
on the fly. May the stories in these pages stoke
this kind of adventure.

WILDSAM
FIELD GUIDES

Our deepest thanks to the many Texans who helped
bring this book to life. Any field guide involves a steady
exchange of ideas and intel, but this one doubly so given
the state's enormous breadth, both in size and cultural
import. Thanks to the dedicated researchers at The
Wittliff Collections, Dolph Briscoe Center for American
History and LBJ Presidential Library. We're grateful for
generosity and insight from Chrissy and Jay Kleberg,
Anne Brookshire, Nicholas Miller, Casey Gerald, Mia
Baxter Smail, Ben Masters, Ferrell Fields, Charlie
Biedenharn, Jim Ward, Mia Carameros and Norbert
Portillo, along with many others—thank you!

WILDSAM FIELD GUIDES™

Published in the United States
by Wildsam Field Guides, Austin, Texas.
Printed in Canada.

ISBN 978-1-4671-9900-1

Design by Alan Kahler
Illustrations by Kelly Colchin

To find more field guides, please visit
www.wildsam.com

CONTENTS

Discover the people and places that tell the story of Texas

ESSENTIALS 007
Trusted intel about geography, lodging and culture,
plus region-by-region expertise

CITIES & TOWNS 019
Profiles and local knowledge about iconic
communities throughout Texas

ALMANAC 035
Archival excerpts, timelines, news clippings
and other historical musings

ROAD TRIPS 063
Routes and recommendations for soulful journeys
through the state

INTERVIEWS 095
Concise and meaningful one-way conversations
with Texans of note

STORIES 119
Original essays and reprinted masterworks
from respected Texas writers

INDEX 147

NOTES 152

WELCOME

LATE JOURNALIST AND PLAYWRIGHT Larry L. King knew well the Texas myth. Raised in a ranch town called Putnam, King lived his adult life in New York and Washington, D.C. He called himself a Texas expatriate. "Texas is my mind's country," King wrote, in 1975 for *Atlantic Monthly*. "The dead past and the living future tie me to it." In the piece, called "Playing Cowboy," King described the folk-heroic Texas, the one of singing creeks and fortune makers on horseback, of the great and wide frontier. "Texas when she was young," as he put it. King knew the foolish drug of nostalgia, but he pushed past the scrub brush still: "For a precious few moments I exist in a time warp: I'm back in Old Texas, under a high sky, where all things are again possible and the wind blows free."

Texas is big. *El Paso, 857 miles* is a real thing. Texas is loaded with stories of bootstrap characters, epic swings from nothing to everything [and back again]. Texas is swagger and thick skin, quick wit and knockout smiles. Bob Wills and Beyoncé, Ann Richards and LBJ. Perhaps most core, Texas possesses a dogged independence. The books may say the state motto is "Friendship," but a truer one is "Don't mess with Texas."

The same year King wrote his essay, Willie Nelson released his outlaw concept album *Red Headed Stranger*. Bigwigs at Columbia Records predicted a bust—"They called it a demo tape," Willie says —but he ignored them. Whiny harmonica, slow guitar, lo-fi Willie on the run. That was his way, and the thing went boom. Number one country album, his first. These are the last words Willie sings on the album: "With no place to hide, I looked in your eyes, and I found myself in you. And I looked to the stars, tried all of the bars, and I've nearly gone up in smoke. Now my hand's on the wheel of something that's real. And I feel like I'm goin' home."

For the better part of the past few years, the eyes of the nation have been on Texas and how Texans treat the stranger on the border. For those people too, this state represents possibility and independence, a new home. The question then: Are these values part of the Texas myth? Or are they its living future? —The Editors

008   *Planning*

009   *Geography and Foodways*

010   *History*

011   *Film, Music and Books*

012   *Lodging*

013   *Parks and Public Lands*

014   *Issues*

015   *Regional Abstracts*

ESSENTIALS

Trusted intel and
traveler info about iconic
statewide culture and practices

PLANNING

TRANSPORT

RAIL
Texas State Railroad
Palestine
texasstaterailroad.net

....

HORSES
Lajitas Stables
Terlingua
lajitasstables.com

....

ROAD BIKE
Mellow Johnny's
Austin & Fort Worth
austin.mellowjohnnys.com

....

RIVER FLOAT
Frio Fergie's River Store
Frio River in Concan
7bluffcabins.com

....

MOTORCYCLE
Eaglerider
McAllen, Austin, DFW
eaglerider.com

....

RANCH PLANE
Trinity Private Jet Charter
Love Field in Dallas
trinityjet.com

....

RV & TRAVEL TRAILER
Outdoorsy
Statewide
outdoorsy.com

CLIMATE
Unpredictable is the forecast.
In the arid West, expect clear
skies and 10 inches of rain a
year, while a trip eastward
yields subtropical humidity
under Spanish moss. Temps
scorch in the six-month
summer, hurricanes in football
season, snow [if you're lucky]
readies you for a bluebonnet
spring.

CALENDAR

JAN	Texas Citrus Fiesta, Mission
FEB	Lone Star Cowboy Poetry Gathering, Alpine
MAR	SXSW and Luck Reunion, Austin, Houston Rodeo
APR	Round Top Antiques Fair Old Settlers Music Festival, Lockhart
MAY	Kerrville Folk Festival
JUN	Watermelon Thump, Luling
JUL	Spring Ho, Lampasas
AUG	Texas Outdoor Musical, Palo Duro Canyon
SEP	Texas State Fair, Dallas World Heritage Festival, San Antonio
OCT	Chinati Foundation Weekend, Marfa
NOV	Ranch Hand Weekend, Kingsville, Texas Book Festival, Austin
DEC	Matagorda Bay Christmas Bird Count

GEOGRAPHY

Notable terrain formations and where to find them.

LIMESTONE SPRINGS

Clear water bubbles through natural openings after passing through filtering chambers. *Comal Springs, New Braunfels*

....

CALICHE BERM

Calcium carbonate deposits lead to sedimentary rock formations ranging from chalky white to pale pink. *Sulfur Springs Draw, Lamesa*

OAK MOTTES

Ancient clusters nurse undergrowth plants and offer shady warrens for deer, turkey and birds. *Brazos Bend State Park, Needville*

....

TUPELO SWAMPS

Slow-moving wetlands; mooring cypress roots submerged, conical "knees" exposed. *Caddo Lake, East Texas*

SKY ISLANDS

Isolated, cooler peaks surrounded by arid desert below with rich mammal and fowl biodiversity. *Davis Mountains, Fort Davis*

....

TIDAL FLATS

Coastal ecosystem fluctuating between saturated and swamped; breeding ground for insects eaten by shore birds. *Mustang Island, Port Aransas*

FOODWAYS

History, culture and tradition in a dish.

Brisket — This succulent cut [#120 in the butcher's book] draws eaters the world over with 12-hour smoke signals. *Smitty's or Kreuz, Lockhart*

Kolache — These downy pastries beckon the Czech roots of Central Texas. Sweet fruit filling or link sausage? One of each, ma'am. *Hruska's, Ellinger*

Enchilada Platter — Your plate is heaping and hot, rice and beans cozied up to the slathered main dish. Tamal as a bonus. *La Fonda on Main, San Antonio*

Chicken-Fried Steak — Circa 1920, this pan-fried beefsteak, topped with milk gravy, pairs well with a nap. *Jacoby's Cafe, Melvin*

HISTORY

1528 ..... Cabeza de Vaca shipwrecked, lives among Karankawa

1685 ..... France raises flag [two of six] near Matagorda Bay

1822 ..... Stephen F. Austin inherits land, becomes colony empresario

1836 ..... Texas gains independence from Mexico after battles of the Alamo [loss], Coleto [loss] and San Jacinto [win]

..... Austin dies on December 27

1874..... Decisive battle at Palo Duro Canyon, the "Last Chief of the Comanche" Quanah Parker surrenders

1878 ..... Bastrop butcher Peter Gill first sells his "barbecued meats and cooked sausages"

1900..... The Great Storm wrecks Galveston on September 8

..... In October, UT beats Oklahoma in first "Red River Rivalry"

1901 ..... Spindletop [Beaumont] erupts, ushers in first oil boom

1932 ..... Port Arthur's Babe Didrikson wins gold at Olympics

1950 ..... Whataburger opens in Corpus Christi

1957 ..... Construction of "Alamo Village" for John Wayne film begins in Brackettville

1951 ..... George H.W. Bush moves family to Midland after Yale

1963 ..... John F. Kennedy assassinated at Dealey Plaza; LBJ sworn in

1965 ..... Houston Astrodome opens, "Eighth Wonder of the World"

1967 ..... Pocket calculator invented by Texas Instruments

1974..... Ten Cadillacs buried outside Amarillo

1976 ..... Barbara Jordan gives keynote at Democratic National Convention

1980..... 83 million Americans tune in to find out "Who Shot J.R.?"

1981 ..... Beyoncé Giselle Knowles born in Houston

1985 ..... "Don't Mess With Texas" Stevie Ray Vaughan TV spot

1990 ..... Ann Richards wins governor's race; loses to George W. Bush in 1994

1993 ..... 51-day "Waco Siege" ends with 76 dead, including David Koresh

1994..... Dallas Cowboys, Super Bowl champs [again]

1996 ..... Statewide licensing of concealed handguns begins

2000..... Enron claims $101 billion revenue, files for bankruptcy in 2001

2015 ..... Rick Perry completes 15-year stretch as governor

2017 ..... Category 4 Hurricane Harvey makes landfall in Texas

MEDIA

FILM	MUSIC
Tree of Life	Bills Wills & His Texas Playboys
The Texas Chain Saw Massacre	Lightin' Hopkins
Giant	Willie Nelson
North Dallas Forty	The Skunks
Hell or High Water	DJ Screw
The Searchers	Selena
Hands on a Hardbody	Dixie Chicks
Boyhood	Los Lonely Boys
No Country for Old Men	Robert Earl Keen
Reality Bites	Kacey Musgraves

BOOKS

☞ The Larry McMurtry Reader: Start with *The Last Picture Show* for small-town Texas; graduate to his Western tome *Lonesome Dove*; finish with Houston-set *Terms of Endearment*.

....

☞ *The Liars' Club* by Mary Karr: This 1995 bestseller ranks way-up-high on best-ever lists, praise due to Karr's poetic journey into her hardscrabble town and family furies.

....

☞ *Borderlands/La Frontera: The New Mestiza* by Gloria Anzaldúa: As a Chicana feminist poet, the exploration of boundaries is fitting in this brilliant work of hybridity.

....

☞ *The Path to Power* by Robert Caro: Book One of his grand political epic drops the reader into LBJ's Hill Country and early ambition, tracking the beginnings of an extraordinary rise.

....

☞ *Places Left Unfinished at the Time of Creation* by John Phillip Santos: A San Antonio writer searches for truth within his family's journey from northern Mexico to South Texas.

....

☞ *God Save Texas* by Lawrence Wright: *The New Yorker* writer [who calls Austin home] studies what really makes Texas tick and poses the high stakes for the future in tumultuous times.

LODGING

ADOBE INN

Indian Lodge

Fort Davis

tpwd.texas.gov

Historic 1930s quarters in remote valley with pool and trail access.

....

HISTORIC ELEGANCE

Hotel Emma

San Antonio

thehotelemma.com

Jewel of the Pearl Brewery deserves every single drop of high praise.

....

BOHEMIAN RETREAT

Rancho Pillow

Round Top

ranchopillow.com

This cool compound sits five miles from the renowned antiques fields.

....

GRAND

The Plaza Hotel

El Paso

plazahotelelpaso.com

Trost-designed high-rise, once home to Liz Taylor, was smartly redone in 2020.

BOUTIQUE

The Carpenter Hotel

Austin

carpenterhotel.com

Old union digs for tradesfolk, now super-hip digs a hop from Barton Springs.

....

LUXURY

The Adolphus

Dallas

adolphus.com

The French Room Bar conjures up way-back boom Texas. Whiskey neat.

....

WEST TEXAS

Gage Hotel

Marathon

gagehotel.com

In a tiny town deep into high desert country, oasis is exactly the word.

....

RANCH

Rocker B Ranch

Graford

exploreranches.com

Yes, this 320-acre spread in the Palo Pinto can be yours— for the weekend.

RIVER BUNGALOW

Frio River Cabins

Leakey

cabinsfrioriver.com

Summer camp memories, just a float down from Garner State Park.

....

BEACH CAMP

Mustang Island State Park

Corpus Christi

tpwd.texas.gov

Sleep under the stars on this skinny barrier island 3,995 acres long.

....

PINEY WOODS

Hotel Ritual

Jacksonville

ritualonmain.com

Wes Anderson would approve of this retreat with spa and luncheonette.

....

EXCLUSIVE

Hotel Saint Cecilia

Austin

hotelsaintcecilia.com

Liz Lambert's peacock-blue riff on where a British rocker would stay.

PARKS AND PUBLIC LANDS

Exemplary entry points into the state's varied landscapes and wilderness.

LOST MAPLES STATE NATURAL AREA
Bandera County, East-West Trail
Sabinal River snakes through rare grove of Uvalde bigtooth maples where fall colors abound.

···

INKS LAKE STATE PARK
Burnet County, Devils Water Hole
Granite trails, cliff jumping, lakeside camping [#333 is best]; one of six in the Highland Lakes chain.

···

GUADALUPE MOUNTAINS NATIONAL PARK
Culberson County, McKittrick Canyon Trail
Four highest peaks at this remote, varied [sand dunes and coniferous forests] park bordering New Mexico.

···

MISSIONS TRAIL
Bexar County, Hike and Bike trail
San Antonio River connects five missions: Concepción, San José, San Juan, Espada and San Antonio de Valero [Alamo].

···

CADDO LAKE STATE PARK
Harrison County, Saw Mill Pond
Maze of bayous inhabited by egrets, herons, American alligators. Equally explorable by boat and foot.

···

GOOSE ISLAND STATE PARK
Aransas County, St. Charles Bay
Home to thousand-year-old "Big Tree"; launching point for anglers [redfish, drum], birders [snowy egret, green heron].

···

MCKINNEY FALLS STATE PARK
Travis County, Upper Falls
Onion Creek rushes over limestone ledges pooling into natural baths; 10 minutes from Austin's Congress Avenue.

ISSUES

Immigration	Texans pride themselves on their cross-cultural communities, a quality under fire with "build the wall" crowing from Washington and a disgraceful crisis inside 184 border detention centers. **EXPERT:** *Jonathan Ryan, CEO of RAICES, legal advocacy group for immigrant families*
Guns	More than a third of Texans own a gun, with 725,000 guns registered [#1 in the U.S.] and over 10,000 dealers. Yet with seven mass shootings in 10 years, gun control laws have loosened. **EXPERT:** *Houston Police Chief Art Acevedo*
Water	Climate change, population growth [led U.S. in 2018-2019], an aging water treatment workforce and erratic regulation leads to threatened aquifers, which supply 60% of the state's water. **EXPERT:** *L'Oreal W. Stepney, Office of Water, Texas Commission of Environmental Quality*
Rural Health Care	Though 1.5 million people live in rural Texas, health care is drying up. At last count, 33 counties have no doctor, and the number of rural hospitals is 50% what it was 50 years ago. Obesity, alcoholism and maternal health are priorities. **EXPERT:** *Holly Jeffreys, Panhandle Family Care Clinic*

STATISTICS

91 .... Meters of denim needed for Big Tex's pants

1,500,000 .... Adobe bricks used in "Happy" Shahan's Alamo replica

30,000 .... Pounds of wildflower seeds purchased by TxDOT annually

61 .... #1 George Strait singles

19,742,267 .... Votes for Ross Perot during his 1992 presidential bid

3 .... Years Paul Cullen spent in prison after poisoning Austin's Treaty Oak

LONE STAR STATE

EST. 1845 MOTTO: *Friendship*

STATE BIRD
NORTHERN MOCKINGBIRD

STATE FLOWER
BLUEBONNET

STATE GEM
TOPAZ

STATE SONG
"TEXAS, OUR TEXAS"

SIX FLAGS OVER TEXAS

Spain

France

Mexico

Republic of Texas

Confederate States

United States

CULTURAL LANDMARKS

San Antonio Missions
UNESCO World Heritage site

Apollo Mission Control Center
Houston

Alibates Flint Quarries
National Monument

Astrodome
Houston

King Ranch
Kingsville

Neiman Marcus Building
Dallas

PINE BELT

WILDFLOWERS
BLUE-EYED GRASS (APRIL)
BIG THICKET NATURE PRESERVE

HIGH SCHOOL FOOTBALL
JACKSONVILLE INDIANS VS
MARSHALL MAVERICKS,
TOMATO BOWL, JACKSONVILLE

RODEO
GLADEWATER ROUND-UP
STARTED IN 1938

SMALL FESTIVAL
Tyler Rose Festival
texasrosefestival.com

CLASSIC RESTAURANT
Florida's Kitchen
Livingston
floridaskitchen.com

LIVE MUSIC
Banita Creek Hall
Nacogdoches
banitacreekhall.com

SCENIC DRIVE
Pineywoods
Autumn Trail
Athens to Palestine

SWIMMING HOLE
Blue Hole
Jasper County
Angelina National Forest

MEMENTO
Hand-thrown mug
throceramics.com

HILL COUNTRY

WILDFLOWERS
INDIAN PAINTBRUSH (MARCH, APRIL)
BALCONES CANYONLANDS NWR

HIGH SCHOOL FOOTBALL
MASON PUNCHERS VS CENTER POINT
PIRATES, PUNCHER DOME, MASON

RODEO
CRIDER'S (HUNT)
PART RODEO, PART DANCE HALL

SMALL FESTIVAL
Lavender Fest
blancolavenderfest.com

CLASSIC RESTAURANT
Cooper's Old Time Pit Bar-B-Que
Llano
coopersbbq.com

LIVE MUSIC
Albert Icehouse
Stonewall
alberttexas.com

SCENIC DRIVE
Willow City Loop
Fredericksburg
County roads public,
land privately owned

SWIMMING HOLE
Hamilton Pool
Highway 71
parks.traviscountytx.gov

MEMENTO
Custom Stetson
Maufrais
maufrais.shop

SOUTH TEXAS

WILDFLOWERS
TEXAS LANTANA (APRIL)
CHOKE CANYON STATE PARK

HIGH SCHOOL FOOTBALL
HANNA EAGLES VS RIVERA RAIDERS,
SAMS MEMORIAL, BROWNSVILLE

RODEO
BUC DAYS (CORPUS CHRISTI)
PART OF PRO RODEO CIRCUIT

SMALL FESTIVAL
Charro Days Fiesta
Brownsville
charrodaysfiesta.com

CLASSIC RESTAURANT
King's Inn
Baffin Bay
kingsinnriviera.com

LIVE MUSIC
Executive Surf Club
Corpus Christi
waterstmarketcc.com

SCENIC DRIVE
Coastal Texas
From Aransas National
Wildlife Refuge TX 35 to 361

SWIMMING HOLE
Boca Chica
Go 23 miles east of Brownsville,
until Hwy 4 hits the beach

MEMENTO
Cuero fragrance
Boyd's of Texas
boydsoftexas.com

PANHANDLE PLAINS

....

⊛ WILDFLOWERS
BASKETFLOWER (JUNE, JULY)
BUFFALO LAKE NWR

🏈 HIGH SCHOOL FOOTBALL
SWEETWATER MUSTANGS VS SNYDER
TIGERS, MUSTANG BOWL, SWEETWATER

🤠 RODEO
BIG SPRING COWBOY REUNION
EIGHT DECADES STRAIGHT, EVERY JUNE

———————————————

SMALL FESTIVAL
Fort Griffin Fandangle
Albany
fortgriffinfandangle.org
....

CLASSIC RESTAURANT
The Bucket
Canadian
[806] 323-8200
....

LIVE MUSIC
Cactus Theatre
Lubbock
cactustheater.com
....

SCENIC DRIVE
Scenic Canyonlands,
Runs 48 miles on Hwy 207
from Claude to Silverton
....

SWIMMING HOLE
Lake Fryer
Hwy 83
Wolf Creek Park
....

MEMENTO
The "Chirping" Crickets on vinyl
Ralph's Records
ralphsrecordstx.com

BIG BEND

....

⊛ WILDFLOWERS
PRICKLY PEAR CACTUS (APRIL)
BIG BEND NATIONAL PARK

🏈 HIGH SCHOOL FOOTBALL
BALMORHEA BEARS VS RANKIN
RED DEVILS, BEAR STADIUM (8-MAN)

🤠 RODEO
WEST OF THE PECOS (PECOS)
SINCE 1883, OLDEST IN THE SPORT

———————————————

SMALL FESTIVAL
Terlingua Chili
Cook-Off
Terlingua
abowlofred.com
....

CLASSIC RESTAURANT
L&J Cafe
El Paso
ljcafe.com
....

LIVE MUSIC
Railroad Blues
Alpine
railroadblues.com
....

SCENIC DRIVE
Davis Mountains
Scenic Loop
From Fort Davis
....

SWIMMING HOLE
San Felipe Springs
Del Rio
....

MEMENTO
Desert Blanket
Garza Marfa
garzamarfa.com

INCLUDING

020	*Houston*
021	*Corpus Christi*
022	*Brownsville*
023	*San Antonio*
024	*Fredericksburg*
025	*Austin*
026	*Waco*
027	*Dallas*
028	*Fort Worth*
029	*Wichita Falls*
030	*Amarillo*
031	*Midland*
032	*Alpine*
033	*El Paso*

CITIES
& TOWNS

Fourteen communities large
and small that capture the
Lone Star State spirit

HOUSTON

POPULATION **2,325,502**

SIZE **669 SQ MILES**

ELEVATION **105 FT**

SUNSHINE **204 DAYS**

COFFEE:
Blacksmith, Catalina, Inversion

BEST DAY OF THE YEAR:
Trail Rides Day

There's an attitude in Houston as unmistakable as the July humidity. Beyoncé called it "H-Town vicious." Food writer John T. Edge dubbed this place "Mutt City." Another clue: The city's rappers coined the term "trill," a combination of "true" and "real." Yes, Houstonians move with purpose and without pretension, but their soft spot is their enormous hometown pride. To see it enshrined, head to WEST ALABAMA ICEHOUSE, an open-air relic of this very-Texas kind of gathering place that dates to pre-fridge days, when you'd buy a block of ice and crack open a beer. Next up, a fajita plate at the original NINFA'S ON NAVIGATION, where in 1973 Ninfa Laurenzo made Texans fall in love with the Tex-Mex classic. Each March, the entire city pulls on their boots for the HOUSTON LIVESTOCK SHOW AND RODEO, a 20-night spectacle of roping contests, live music and fried food on a stick. Don't miss the mutton bustin'. Houston is also cosmic country, home to the JOHNSON SPACE CENTER, where NASA Mission Control set its sights on the stars in the 1960s. This museum makes the moonshot history feel more personal. In many ways, this is the Houston trademark: hefty ambition comes down-to-earth.

LOCAL TO KNOW

"The Heights is family-oriented, a small community, not what people think of when they think of Houston. I love Coltivare. Go on a Sunday night to wind down. A cocktail in their garden, chicken wings and cacio e pepe: That's my go-to."
— TRAVIS WEAVER, founder Manready Mercantile

CORPUS CHRISTI

POPULATION **326,554**

SIZE **452.2 SQ MILES**

ELEVATION **7 FT**

SUNSHINE **223 DAYS**

COFFEE:
Eleanor's, Green Light Coffee, Coffee Waves

BEST DAY OF THE YEAR:
State Surfing Championship

In Texas' only city by the sea, wild nature and culture converge. The pristine Padre Island National Seashore, the longest undeveloped barrier island in the world, shows off the raw beauty of the Texas coast. Go early to find seashells aglow in morning light. In summer, join a sea turtle release to watch hatchlings totter into the Gulf. Back in town, check out the Philip Johnson-designed ART MUSEUM OF SOUTH TEXAS, particularly the archives of Dorothy Hood, arguably the mother of modern art in Texas. Hit Hester's, the museum café, for a lunch with bay views. Cruise down scenic OCEAN DRIVE, top-down, with a stop at Oleander Point at Cole Park to check out the hotshots of the kite and windsurfing scene, or get out on the water yourself through WATERDOG, a paddleboard yoga studio with floating classes near the yacht club. The Texas Surf Museum and WATER STREET OYSTER BAR [same owner] continue Corpus' beach-town note. But perhaps its most significant refrain, as locals will tell you, is Selena Quintanilla-Pérez, the beloved and still mourned cumbia star. Her untimely death shook the city in 1995. Fans pay homage at her seaside gravesite, the bronze statue near Harrison's Landing and the small but intimate SELENA MUSEUM.

LOCAL TO KNOW

"The Corpus music scene is a mashup. Boozerz is my weird secret hang-out, the only place I go on the Southside. It's a punk rock bar with bikers, gangsters and nurses. And everybody's cool."
—HORACIO "EL DUSTY" OLIVEIRA, neo-cumbia DJ,
owner Produce music studio

BROWNSVILLE

POPULATION **183,299**

SIZE **82 SQ MILES**

ELEVATION **33 FT**

SUNSHINE **223 DAYS**

COFFEE:
7th & Park, El Hueso de Fraile, Angelita's Casa de Cafe

BEST DAY OF THE YEAR:
Charro Days' Baile del Sol Street Dance

This breezy city on the southern tip of the state offers an authentic look into cross-cultural life between Mexico and Texas. The border is often two places at once. Read up on life in Brownsville from fiction writer Oscar Cásares, who grew up in the Rio Grande Valley, and whose celebrated short stories and novels transcend the political. The Saturday morning FARMERS' MARKET is another way to see into real life in Brownsville. Local producers and growers [and live guitar players] set up at Linear Park in the Mitte Cultural District, also adjacent to the HISTORIC BATTLEFIELD TRAIL, 8 miles of reclaimed railroad tracks turned hike-and-bike. SEVENTH & PARK, a smart coffee and full-service bike shop, rings the bell of a new day for Brownsville small business. Similarly, the Neapolitan pie bar DODICI PIZZA & WINE, steps from the historic Market Square, has become a locals' favorite since firing its Italian-made oven in 2018. Dodici owner Trey Mendez was elected mayor in June 2019, a positive sign of things to come for Brownsville. Long pigeonholed as a dusty county seat and gateway to birding country, this South Texas city is now positioned to reimagine, for the state and beyond, the unique potential of a border city.

LOCAL TO KNOW

"Brownsville is unique because there are three border crossings within city limits. I think of it like the tide: People flow in in the morning and out in the evening. Most interactions you have here, the person you're talking to will either be one generation removed from Mexico or still have family there."

— GRAHAM SEVIER-SCHULTZ, owner 7th & Park

SAN ANTONIO

POPULATION **1,532,233**

SIZE **465 SQ MILES**

ELEVATION **650 FT**

SUNSHINE **220 DAYS**

COFFEE:
Rosella, Theory Coffee Company

BEST DAY OF THE YEAR:
Last Friday in April; Battle of the Flowers Parade

The San Antonio River runs for 240 miles and straight through the heart of the Bexar County seat. For centuries of dwellers, from Comanche to Spanish, the river has been like a crystal-blue bloodline for the city. A throughline, literally and figuratively. Given the storied import of the waterway, we suggest you start at the beginning, its historic source visible through a limestone well at HEADWATERS SANCTUARY. Enjoy Brackenridge Park, then make your way to the recently renovated WITTE MUSEUM, where the natural and prehistoric stories of Texas come alive. Continue your riverside promenade, an organic and industrial mix, where you'll amble upon the rightfully celebrated Pearl development, with its jewel centerpiece, HOTEL EMMA. There's no finer hotel in Texas. Settle in as you gather lawn picnic provisions from BAKERY LORRAINE, Larder, the weekend farmers market and High Street Wine Co. Tempted to linger, keep going downriver to the iconic [and touristy] classic River Walk loop. Throwbacks Esquire Tavern and CASA RIO shine brightest. Remember the Alamo but don't forget its four sister missions, including MISSION SAN JOSÉ, whose ornate rose window is worth the trip itself.

LOCAL TO KNOW

"My favorite stretch of the river is the Hot Wells ruins site. It's this old resort with thermal baths. Prior to the Great Depression it was a destination for people from all over the U.S., including movie stars. Recently, Bexar County preserved the ruins and created a public park that can be accessed through the river."

— KELLY O'CONNOR, collage-installation artist

FREDERICKSBURG

POPULATION **11,446**

SIZE **8.6 SQ MILES**

ELEVATION **1,693 FT**

SUNSHINE **224 DAYS**

COFFEE:
Caliche Coffee Bar & Ranch Road Roasters,
Woerner Warehouse

BEST DAY OF THE YEAR:
Bluebonnets on the first Sunday in April

Charming and chiseled, Fredericksburg's limestone architecture, über-strollable downtown and surrounding wineries have long made it a daytrip destination. But a new generation of residents—many who chose to leave behind bigger cities—are carving out new life in this historic German enclave. Two paths for lodging: Outside of town, Contigo Ranch's stylish cottages hit a Marfa note on 300-plus acres. In town, the restored ALBERTINA HOUSE overlooks Main Street, a quick walk to morning coffee and biscuits at Emma + Ollie bakeshop café. Down the road, BLACKCHALK HOME AND LAUNDRY stocks modern home goods and Turkish rugs. For a walkable wine crawl, head to bottleshop and bar LA BERGERIE; owners John and Evelyn Washburne also run German dinner favorite Otto's. Next stop, PONTOTOC VINEYARD WEINGARTEN, where locals linger at picnic tables in the stonewalled courtyard. Looking for a longneck instead? On weekends, the PECAN GROVE STORE, an old Sinclair gas station, serves up massive "Dino Burgers," while Texas-country bands amp up a Saturday night. Best way to see all those wildflowers? Grab a set of wheels at Jack & Adam's Bicycles and cycle the 13-mile Willow City Loop.

LOCAL TO KNOW

"We like to hunt for old dirt backroads. You always see something interesting—a newborn fawn or a rattlesnake crawling across the road. On Saturdays, by late afternoon, you can smell the backyard barbecue smoke drifting through the neighborhood."
— CLAUDIA AND ROBERT FEUGE, artists

AUSTIN

POPULATION **950,715**

SIZE **305 SQ MILES**

ELEVATION **489 FT**

SUNSHINE **289 DAYS**

COFFEE:
*Jo's, Flat Track, Radio, Houndstooth,
Better Half, Cosmic, Medici*

BEST DAY OF THE YEAR:
Summer solstice at Barton Springs

Austin's attraction still glows red-hot like the neon signs lining South Congress Avenue. Its reputation as a free-spirited live music and breakfast taco oasis continues to add 100 people to the population every day, but there's a gentle, easygoing side to the city. A perfect, peaceful day starts with a Tex-Mex breakfast [migas or huevos rancheros] at locally loved greasy spoon CISCO'S CAFE. Amble around the University of Texas campus toward the Blanton Museum of Art, home to ELLSWORTH KELLY'S "AUSTIN", a universalist chapel where rainbow light dances across the walls, an architectural nod to the artist's paintings. Or take in nature's own color theory with a sunset kayak rent from ROWING DOCK, just north of Zilker Park on the turquoise LADY BIRD LAKE. This is a perfect floating skyline view. For dinner eat barside at JUNE'S, a sunny all-day cafe with spot-on Sunday evening Indian fare, or Mediterranean-influenced LAUNDERETTE, where it's best to end your meal with a birthday cake ice cream sandwich. Both examples of Austin's newer wave of neighborhood spots. The best of Old Austin? Piano bar DONN'S DEPOT, strung in Christmas lights no matter the month, hosts old-timer musicians nightly with a judgment-free dance floor.

LOCAL TO KNOW

*"On a typical Saturday we're in a neighborhood park or a
community garden, or over at 11th and Navasota painting a
mural. We work to remedy urbanization with beautification.
It brings the community together."*

— RAASIN MCINTOSH, olympian, founder, Raasin in the Sun

WACO

POPULATION **138,183**

SIZE **95.5 SQ MILES**

ELEVATION **470 FT**

SUNSHINE **230 DAYS**

COFFEE:
Pinewood Coffee, Common Grounds,
 Magnolia Press Coffee Co

BEST DAY OF THE YEAR:
Brazos Nights

Waco has become synonymous with shiplap thanks to its recent revitalization brought about by home reno wunder-duo [and city cheerleaders] Chip and Joanna Gaines. But this bustling college town, and the original fount of Dr Pepper, has always had good bones. THE WACO SUSPENSION BRIDGE, repurposed as a pedestrian walkway between two modernized city parks on either side of the Brazos River, was the longest single-span connector in the West when it was built in 1870. Now paddlers steer their stand-up boards and kayaks underneath through the BOSQUE BLUFFS. Another salvaged landmark, the WACO HIPPODROME THEATRE, circa 1914, has added a hopping bar in the lobby for films and concerts. No historical marker lies at the site of the Branch Davidian siege, but still, those curious about the tragedy drive out to see the now-empty field where the compound stood. The city's lesser-known renaissance has been in barbecue with the brick-and-mortar establishments of food truck favorites GUESS FAMILY BARBECUE and HELBERG BARBECUE. Both serve peppery, tender brisket on butcher paper-lined trays. Walk downtown to see the new, design-minded shops like WILDLAND SUPPLY CO. and GATHER with collections of hard-to-find apothecary brands and hand-thrown pottery. To live a full day in the Magnolia lifestyle [if an afternoon at THE SILOS isn't enough], book a stay at one of three Gaineses renovated properties, STAY, with a hotel on the horizon.

LOCAL TO KNOW

"I came to Waco for school, but stayed for community. This place draws you in. The Woodway park side of the lake is our favorite swimming spot, and usually you get the place to yourself."
— JARED HIMSTEDT, head distiller Balcones Distilling

DALLAS

POPULATION **1,345,047**

SIZE **386 SQ MILES**

ELEVATION **430 FT**

SUNSHINE **234 DAYS**

COFFEE:
Cultivar, Ascension, Bonton Farms Coffee Shop

BEST DAY OF THE YEAR:
Thanksgiving Day with the Dallas Cowboys

Big D built its glitzy reputation via its oil, gas and banking pioneers, but a creative surge in the city is rising in welcome relief against the buttoned-up edges. There's a youthful energy pushing against what outsiders might consider as typical Dallas. Before taking the town, snag a pair of fashion-forward boots at MIRON CROSBY'S Highland Park Village salon. Downtown ready, peek the contemporary installations at HALL ARTS HOTEL, which sits alongside heritage property The Joule and recently restored midcentury gem THE STATLER. Just west of downtown, CRAIGHEAD GREEN GALLERY represents an impressive and wide-ranging array of artists; look for his annual "New Texas Talent" exhibition. It's just a quick drive to the 1920s-era BISHOP ARTS DISTRICT, home to tiny bistro Lucia and indie bookstore—with a bar inside—THE WILD DETECTIVES. While you're there, swing by MARCEL MARKET for your fill of French fashion and foodstuffs. In East Dallas, the word is out on Misti Norris' PETRA & THE BEAST, a former gas station whipping out menus that evolve daily. Walk-ins only Wednesday through Friday. End on a strong note, just a few blocks from Fair Park, at R.L.'S BLUES PALACE #2 [Thursday-Sunday], home to DJ and blues artist R.L. Griffin.

LOCAL TO KNOW

*"Jimmy's Food Store makes the best sandwiches.
I go for a weekday lunch muffuletta or meatball sub. I always
make sure to grab their frozen dough and sauce so
I can make homemade pizza for dinner."*
— CHRISTINE VISNEAU, curator Commerce Goods + Supply

FORT WORTH

POPULATION **895,008**

SIZE **349 SQ MILES**

ELEVATION **653 FT**

SUNSHINE **222 DAYS**

COFFEE:
Sons of Liberty, Craftwork Coffee Co., Avoca Coffee

BEST DAY OF THE YEAR:
March 20 [spring begins], Joe T. Garcia's patio

Fort Worth is one of the country's fast-growing cities; despite the boom, there's still plenty of pride in Fort Worth's history—after all, it's the place "Where the West Begins." You can catch a glimpse of Cowtown's past twice daily in the STOCKYARDS NATIONAL HISTORIC DISTRICT, where Longhorn ramble down East Exchange Avenue [11:30 a.m., 4 p.m.], or at the Stockyards Championship Rodeo, the country's oldest indoor [and only year-round] rodeo. Next up, you'll want to see where Fort Worth faces forward: The Kimbell Art Museum houses globe- and era-spanning masterworks in an iconic Louis Kahn edifice; nearby, the MODERN ART MUSEUM OF FORT WORTH, in a Tadao Ando-designed building, seems to float—along with its punchy collection—weightlessly atop a reflecting pond. After "feeding the eye," rest at the SINCLAIR FORT WORTH, a new hotel occupying a historic 1930 art deco building. For dinner, hit Heim Barbecue, a craft BBQ upstart; BENITO'S for authentic chiles rellenos in a no-frills Mexican joint; or go upscale at farm-to-table Ellerbe Fine Foods. In the morning, walk off the calories—and catch a glimpse of the city's pastoral past—at the FORT WORTH NATURE CENTER & REFUGE, where 20 miles of trails wend past a herd of wild bison.

LOCAL TO KNOW

"Fort Worth used to be conservative and quiet. A few years ago you started seeing sparks. I like checking out Shipping & Receiving, a cool warehouse bar with live music, and GDT Studios in River East, a space that puts on really well-done art and music shows."
— NOEL VIRAMONTES, co-owner Fort Worth Blackhouse

WICHITA FALLS

POPULATION **104,576**

SIZE **70.1 SQ MILES**

ELEVATION **948 FT**

SUNSHINE **240 DAYS**

COFFEE:
Hook & Ladder

BEST DAY OF THE YEAR:
Nine days before Labor Day,
Hotter'N Hell Hundred cycling race

Wichita Falls sits on the edge of the Oklahoma border, just south of the Red River, peering up into the Great Plains. It makes sense, then, that this was once a major railway stop and terminus for cowboys driving their stock North. It carries its cowtown charm, albeit with some 20th-century polish. There are plenty of lodging options for those who are just passing through [many are due to Sheppard Air Force Base], but the HARRISON HOUSE bed-and-breakfast, built in 1920 and featuring classic décor, is just right. You'll find a surprising amount of Greek culture here, with no-frills HIBISCUS CAFÉ and upscale bistro Salt & Pepper providing the best opportunities to enjoy Mediterranean flavors. For a taste of the city's Western heritage, pull on your Tony Lamas and head to a refreshed downtown. Yes, swing by the "World's Littlest Skyscraper," but then grab a Numb Chuck IPA at Matt Bitsche's WICHITA FALLS BREWING and head to THE IRON HORSE PUB, where you'll catch folksy crooners like Charley Crockett and Fort Defiance. Don't cool your heels for too long, though. Nearby, lakes like ARROWHEAD, Wichita and Kickapoo offer dramatic trails to hike or bike [some of the best in the state] and lots of hungry fish for anglers from beginner to pro.

LOCAL TO KNOW

"P2 is one of only three places in Texas where you can drive up, sit in your car, order a pitcher of beer, drink it in your car and drive away. It's crazy. There are always rumors they might lose their grandfather clause."

— BRENDAN BELL, real estate agent, worship leader

AMARILLO

POPULATION **199,924**

SIZE **90.3 SQ MILES**

ELEVATION **3,605 FT**

SUNSHINE **259 DAYS**

COFFEE:
Palace Coffee Co, Roasters [*Georgia St.*]

BEST DAY OF THE YEAR:
First Saturday in June,
"Texas Outdoor Musical" opener

Amarillo may be something of a mystery, even to many Texans. A historic cattle trail stop, its remote location is on the south end of the Great Plains, near the winding bends of PALO DURO CANYON. This prairie metropolis, however, has seen a strikingly independent attitude emerge, making it more than just a line in a George Strait song, but a genuine hotbed of music and art, home to red-dirt rockers like Joe Ely and Jimmie Dale Gilmore, and the stark weirdness of the CADILLAC RANCH, a High Plains Stonehenge of half-buried luxury cars. When diving into this thoroughly Western part of Texas, skip the temptation of the famous 72-ounce steak challenge at a certain local tourist trap, and instead opt for something truly hearty and homemade at HOFFBRAU STEAK & GRILL HOUSE or sophisticated at OHMS Cafe & Bar downtown. Your best bet for a pleasant stroll—lined, of course, by restaurants and watering holes—is the 6th Street Antique Mall, a historic collection of businesses stuffed to the gills with cooler-than-Grandma's-attic finds. For those trying to fit in with the locals, a trip to the WEST TEXAS WESTERN STORE, with locations in Canyon and Amarillo, is sure to help you find the perfect cowboy hat. If you're not camping nearby [and you should], hang your hat at THE BARFIELD, Amarillo's first boutique hotel, elegantly housed in the city's first skyscraper, built in 1927.

LOCAL TO KNOW

"This is the big city made up of all the people in the Panhandle—farmers,
ranchers, oil men, bankers and feedlot guys—everybody in between.
When you get outside of town, it's easy to find yourself all alone."
— WILL HOLTON, oil and gas land manager J-Brex Co.

MIDLAND

POPULATION 142,344

SIZE 71.5 SQ MILES

ELEVATION 2,782 FT

SUNSHINE 261 DAYS

COFFEE:
Brew St., Higher Grounds

BEST DAY OF THE YEAR:
Midland-Lee football game; day-of barbecue thrown by both baseball teams

The gateway to far West Texas pops out of nowhere on the impossibly flat Permian Basin, one of the world's richest oil and gas territories. *Texas Monthly*'s recent podcast "Boomtown" captures the high highs and low lows of oil with insightful storytelling. Look beyond the sea of pump jacks to the surprisingly youthful energy of Midland's downtown. Start at the MIDLAND DOWNTOWN FARMERS MARKET, a Saturday tradition on the Museum of the Southwest grounds providing handcrafted jewelry and soaps, freshly roasted coffee beans and local honey. Then make a beeline for MICRO MARKET, a cluster of tiny shops worth mining for florals at Velvet Mesquite; doughnuts at Sisterdough; and hand-painted scarves by Mary Lambeth. Book your seat at OPAL'S TABLE, where fried oysters Rockefeller, ribeye with truffle butter and a substantial whiskey selection make this downtown's posh dinner spot. Your destination for small plates of tuna tartare and blackened shrimp skewers paired with flights of craft beer is Butter, just north of downtown. And that's close to THE BLUE DOOR, a cozy place for the proper nightcap. Rest up between adventures at Cedar Social, a guesthouse less than five minutes from downtown and a nice launch pad for beholding unexpected natural wonders at I20 WILDLIFE PRESERVE.

LOCAL TO KNOW

"We take out-of-towners to the Petroleum Museum, because in some way, we are all in the oil business. It's where you learn the story of our city." — SUSIE HITCHCOCK-HALL, owner Susie's South Forty Confections

ALPINE

POPULATION **6,020**

SIZE **4.7 SQ MILES**

ELEVATION **4,475 FT**

SUNSHINE **247 DAYS**

COFFEE:
Cedar Coffee & Supply, Plaine

BEST DAY OF THE YEAR:
Viva Big Bend Music Festival

Since Marfa gets all the ink, many are surprised to find out that Alpine is actually the biggest hub in the Big Bend region. The town began as a railroad stop on the Southern Pacific—Amtrak's *Sunset Limited* still breezes through—but really arrived with the founding of the school that would become Sul Ross State University, in 1920. To immerse yourself, set up camp at the HOLLAND HOTEL or its sister lodge, The Maverick Inn, then spend some time exploring the MUSEUM OF THE BIG BEND, on the Sul Ross campus, which spans the region's history from cowboys all the way back to the dinosaur days. The Sul Ross campus is also the site of the annual LONESTAR COWBOY POETRY GATHERING each spring, where high and lonesome wordsmiths ply their pastime; carry your literary inspiration downtown to FRONT STREET BOOKS, a few doors up from Judy's Bread & Breakfast. Sports fans of any stripe should check out an Alpine Cowboys baseball game at KOKERNOT FIELD, built in 1947 and modeled after Wrigley. Expect bigger cloudscapes and smaller crowds. Come evening time, dine on some elevated cowboy cuisine at REATA, then take in some live music at Railroad Blues. Stay in town as long as you want—that national park down the road isn't going anywhere.

LOCAL TO KNOW

"Three out of five mornings on the drive to work, I'll see something most people might never catch a glimpse of. This week I saw a moon dog around a full moon; a few days ago, 11 bull elk. Last week it was a bobcat."

— GARY DUNSHEE, owner Big Bend Saddlery

EL PASO

POPULATION **682,669**

SIZE **256.3 SQ MILES**

ELEVATION **3740 FT**

SUNSHINE **297 DAYS**

COFFEE:
Savage Goods, District, Eloise

BEST DAY OF THE YEAR:
*Saturday before Thanksgiving,
WinterFest first light*

Felicidades. You made it 862 miles across the state to its western star, the Sun City. El Paso rises from the Chihuahuan Desert, hemmed in by the Franklin Mountains to the north and the Rio Grande to the south. There are echoes here of San Antonio's spirit and Fort Worth's western sophistication, highlighted in the EL PASO MUSEUM OF ART, the most important art institution within a 250-mile radius. Curators have built an impressive collection of borderland works from Texas and Mexico. Just four blocks east is ELEMI, a modern Mexican restaurant where meaty suadero tacos are plated alongside vegan discada de verduras. For green chile classics, locals rightfully swear by L&J CAFE and Carlos & Mickey's. A common reaction to El Paso is that its beauty is less showy, more effortless. With white walls and a beehive bell tower, the YSLETA MISSION is the city's holy center, as well as the state's oldest mission. And from Rim Road's TOM LEA UPPER PARK, the city is bathed nightly in desert-air sunmelt. When the sun does drop, dance on over to THE TAP BAR AND RESTAURANT, circa 1956, or mosey across the border to the margarita-famous KENTUCKY CLUB. This well-worn route between Mexico and Texas is the defining characteristic of El Paso, a timeless passage that, for residents, has blurred borderlines and created common ground.

LOCAL TO KNOW

"Hueco Tanks is a mecca. The season starts in October and ends in February. The climbers line up at 5 a.m. to get first dibs; they have rock ranches where you can pitch a tent or rent a bed."
— MARINA MONSISVAIS, founder Barracuda PR, KTEP radio host

036   *Barbara Jordan & Ann Richards*

037   *Blue Chippers of Note*

039   *Chili Recipe*

040   *Texas Music timeline*

042   *Juneteenth*

043   *Wildcatters*

044   *JFK Assassination*

046   *Bum Steer timeline*

047   *Dr. Pepper & Whataburger*

048   *Spindletop*

051   *LBJ & Darrell Royal*

052   *Chief Quanah Parker*

053   *Boot Maker lexicon*

054   *The Great Storm*

055   *Mary Kay*

056   *Texas Rangers*

058   *Cabeza de Vaca*

060   *J. Frank Dobie letters*

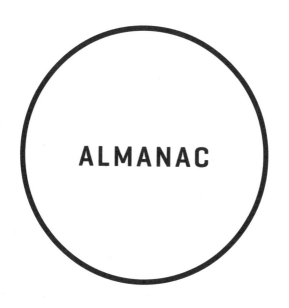

ALMANAC

A deep dive into the cultural heritage
of Texas through news clippings,
timelines, nomenclature and other
historical hearsay

TRAILBLAZERS

*Barbara Jordan and Ann Richards were teachers,
politicians, contemporaries and pioneers. In a state
whose mythology is largely one of the white male, their
presence and words mattered. They still do.*

BARBARA JORDAN

There was a long drouth in the Texas senate for Negro representation. 1883 was a long time ago and, consequently, when I got to the Senate it created a bit of a stir, understandably. I became a part of the sight-seeing tours ... "Who Speaks for the Negro?" Well, I'll answer that question—no one. No one can. You see, the Negro stands silhouetted against a thriving and abundant America and his presence, his very presence on the American scene, speaks for itself ... He wants you to hear him, understand his condition. He feels that if you do this—if you really listen to him as he speaks through his presence and understand his condition—he feels that you'll save him. And that in the process of saving him you will also save this country. And in the process of saving this country you save yourselves.

*Who Speaks for the Negro,
May 27, 1968*

ANN RICHARDS

I was born during the Depression in a little community just outside Waco ... I can remember summer nights when we'd put down what we called a Baptist pallet, and we listened to the grown-ups talk ... I have one nearly perfect granddaughter named Lily. And when I hold that grandbaby, I feel the continuity of life that unites us, that binds generation to generation, that ties us with each other ... I wonder if she'll ever believe that there was a time when blacks could not drink from public water fountains, when Hispanic children were punished for speaking Spanish in the public schools and women couldn't vote. I think of all the political fights I've fought and all the compromises I've had to accept as part payment. And I think of all the small victories that have added up to national triumphs.

*Democratic National Convention
keynote address, July 18, 1988*

BLUE CHIPPERS OF NOTE

JOHN DREW "BOODY" JOHNSON *Waco High*, 1921-23 Scored all 13 points in 1922 state championship; drop-kicking phenom, too.

....

Y.A. TITTLE *Marshall High*, 1941-44 QB's undefeated '44 season launched him to LSU, later, NY Giants and two NFL MVPs.

....

DOAK WALKER *Highland Park*, 1941-44 Before Heisman win, Cotton Bowl acclaim, halfback was a five-sport HS multitasker.

....

KEN HALL *Sugar Land High*, 1950-53 Career rushing [11,232 yards] held U.S. record until 2012; 520 yards on 11 carries in one game.

....

JERRY LEVIAS *Herbert High*, 1962-65 Torched rivals in HS, quarterback for SMU, helped integrate Southwest Conference.

....

EARL CAMPBELL *John Tyler High*, 1970-73 Known as the "Tyler Rose," led '73 team to 4A HS championship; UT's first Heisman.

....

ERIC DICKERSON *Sealy High*, 1975-78 The #1 national prospect and future NFL star ran for 296 yards and 4 touchdowns in state title game.

....

VINCE YOUNG *Madison High*, 1998-2001 Amassed nearly 4,000 yards as a HS senior in front of 40,000-strong Astrodome crowds.

....

JOHNATHAN GRAY *Aledo High*, 2008-11 Scored 205 touchdowns in HS—then a national record—before injuries derailed his career.

....

KYLER MURRAY *Allen High*, 2012-15 Two-time MaxPreps player of the year, 42-0 as starting QB, racked up three state titles.

> *Since 2000, coach Monica Aldama and her Navarro College Cheer Team, have won 14 of the past 19 NCA National Championships. The 38-member team [24 men, 14 women] are known for its high-flying stunts, pyramids, stunts and intricate formations. Its 2020 Netflix series has won universal acclaim.*

WILDFLOWERS

The Wildflower Protection Act [1933] was written to broadly prohibit the picking of any "shrub, vine, flower or moss," on privately owned or publicly held land. Despite its 1973 repeal, the myth endured and narrowed; parents continue to scold bluebonnet-picking children with lawbreaking threats. The indigo bloom, and a multitude of native blossoms, can be viewed March-May, statewide.

....

TEXAS BLUEBONNET *Lupinus texensis* —Cones of clustered cobalt blooms beckon springtime family photos year after year.

FIREWHEEL *Gaillardia pulchella*—Tomato-red blooms rimmed in sunny yellow with toothed edges; thrives in brutal heat.

PINK EVENING PRIMROSE *Oenothera speciose*—Delicate pink cups with butter-colored centers; petals open at dusk and close in the dawn.

TEXAS INDIAN PAINTBRUSH *Castilleja indivisa*—Ignites prairies in fiery crimson; usurps the roots of nearby plants to grow.

WINECUP *Callirhoe involucrata*—Deep coupes in shades of sangria that typically emerge from singular, slender stalks.

ANTELOPE HORN *Asclepias asperula*—Velvety, thick leaves with creamy, curved seedpods; provides food, hosts larvae for monarchs.

WHITE PRICKLYPOPPY *Argemone albiflora*—Ruffled, coffee filter-like blossoms; oily seeds used to make WWII-era alternative lubricant.

RAIN LILY *Cooperia pedunculata*—Flared trumpeting flowers in white and iridescent pink; appears after heavy rains.

BLACKFOOT DAISY *Melampodium leucanthum*—Mustard pom-pom centers encircled by milky petals; produces honeyed fragrance.

HORSEMINT *Monarda citriodora*—Lavender, feathery cowlicks; also known as lemon beebalm.

TEXAS CHILI

Every October, the population of the tiny border town of Terlingua triples when chiliheads from across the globe set up their kettles for the Terlingua International Chili Championship. Houston's Cindy Reed is the competition's only two-time winner. Find her recipe below.

(1) 2 LBS beef chuck tender
cut into 3/8-in cubes
1 TSP cooking oil
1 TBSP dark chili powder
2 TSP granulated garlic

In a three-quart heavy saucepan, add the above ingredients while browning the meat.

....

(2) 8 OZ can of tomato sauce
14 1/2 OZ can of
beef broth
1 TSP chicken bouillon
granules
1 TSP jalapeño powder
1 TBSP onion powder
2 TSP garlic powder
1/2 TSP red pepper
1 TSP white pepper
16 OZ spring water
1 TBSP dark chili powder
2 serrano peppers
1/2 TSP salt

Combine sauce, broth and seasonings. Add to beef mixture.

Bring to a boil, reduce heat, simmer for 1-1/2 hours, float 2 serrano peppers.

....

(3) 1 TBSP paprika
1 PKG Sazon seasoning
[msg]
1 TSP onion powder
1 TSP garlic powder
1/2 TSP white pepper
5 TBSP medium and dark
chili powders

Combine seasonings, add to beef mixture. Bring to a boil, reduce heat, simmer for 20 minutes. You may add water or beef broth for consistency. Remove serrano peppers when they become soft.

....

(4) 2 TSP cumin
1/8 TSP salt

Add above ingredients. Simmer for 10 minutes.

The Texas Chili Parlor opened its doors in 1976; order a mezcal-made Mad Dog margarita alongside your bowl of red. 1409 Lavaca St, Austin.

TEXAS MUSIC

A brief timeline of iconic moments and sounds in the state's musicology.

1903	UT band member writes "Eyes of Texas" lyrics
1917	Blind Lemon Jefferson moves to Deep Ellum in Dallas
1919	Oil driller Orbie Lee Orbison [Vernon] gives guitar to 6-year-old son, Roy
1928	"Lark of the Border" Lydia Mendoza makes first recording
1934	Swingman Bob Wills [regretfully] moves his Playboys to Tulsa
1949	Goree Carter's "Rock Awhile" record debuts
1970	Armadillo World Headquarters opens; second only to Astrodome in Lone Star sales
1971	Janis Joplin's "Me and Bobby McGee" debuts; lyrics by Brownsville's Kris Kristofferson
1973	Jerry Jeff Walker records *¡Viva Terlingua!* in Luckenbach
1974	*Austin City Limits* tapes pilot with Willie Nelson; faux skyline appears in '82
1975	Stoney Ridge band hangs flyer, ag-science student George Strait auditions, lands the gig
1982	*NYT* calls Lightnin' Hopkins the greatest influence on rock guitarists ever
1983	Willie and Merle Haggard cover Townes Van Zandt's "Pancho and Lefty"
1990	Texas Tornados fusion band, led by Flaco Jiménez and Doug Sahm, debuts
1990	Houston's Girls Tyme group forms, includes 9-year-old Beyoncé Knowles
1995	Selena murdered by business manager
1997	Neo-soul artist Erykah Badu [Dallas] releases *Baduizm*
2000	Remix master DJ Screw unexpectedly dies in Houston studio
2006	Famed nightclub owner Clifford Antone dies in Austin
2007	Dixie Chicks' "Not Ready to Make Nice" wins Grammy for Record and Song of the Year
2013	Beyoncé's eponymous album drops with zero promotion, sells 5 million copies
2019	Kacey Musgraves [Golden] wins full sweep [Grammy, ACM, CMA]

JUNETEENTH

On June 19, 1865, Union troops landed in Galveston with a message delivered by General Gordon Granger: "In accordance with a proclamation from the Executive of the United States, all slaves are free." Felix Haywood, a former slave born near San Antonio, was 20 at the time.

Everybody went wild. We all felt like heroes, and nobody had made us that way but ourselves. We were free. Just like that, we were free. It didn't seem to make the whites mad, either. They went right on giving us food just the same. Nobody took our homes, but right off colored folks started on the move. They seemed to want to get closer to freedom, so they knew what it was—like it was a place or a city. We knew freedom was on us but we didn't know what was to come with it. We thought we were going to get rich like the white folks, because we were stronger and knew how to work, and the whites didn't, and we didn't have to work for them any more. But it didn't turn out that way. We soon found out that freedom could make folks proud but it didn't make them rich. *Excerpted from* The Slave Narratives of Texas, *edited by Ron Tyler and Lawrence R. Murphy*

BASEBALL

All respect to Nolan Ryan, but the greatest Texas pitching phenom was a lefty you've likely never heard of.

David Clyde is a left-handed fastball pitcher whose achievements at Westchester High—an 18-0 record in his senior year with an earned run average of 0.18 and 328 strikeouts in 148 innings—were trumpeted throughout Texas. The first player selected in the June 5 major league draft, he had been judged by virtually every scout who saw him as the finest schoolboy pitcher in the nation. He was signed by the Rangers to a contract that called for a bonus of approximately $125,000 and a free college education. He is a teen-ager of extraordinary tact and maturity, one who is humble, courteous and agreeably respectful of his elders. He has curly brown hair, wide blue eyes and a bashful smile. He is 6'1" and he weighs a muscular 190. A paragon of this sort does not just slip into the Rangers' starting rotation; he enters the lists like a knight-errant.—*Sports Illustrated*, 1973

GLENN MCCARTHY

In his prime, the wildcatter had 400 oil-producing wells, was the architect of Houston's "largest in the U.S." Shamrock Hotel and even inspired James Dean's fictional Jett Rink in Giant. *In a state where fortunes are made and lost, McCarthy's penchant for bravado and risk was a step above.*

King of the Wildcatters
TIME
February 13, 1950

If it were possible to cap the human ego like a gas well, and to pipe off its more volatile byproducts as fuel, Houston's multi-millionaire wildcatter Glenn McCarthy could heat a city the size of Omaha with no help at all … As it is, the works and pomps which Glenn McCarthy has raised in honor of McCarthy have taken a more solid form. There is McCarthy's Houston mansion, a white-pillared, $700,000 pile surrounded by vast lawns and trees bearded with Spanish moss. There is the 15,000-acre ranch on which he admires his blooded cattle and occasionally shoots deer, goats and turkeys. There is McCarthy's Colosadium [so far, only on paper], a 110,000-seat stadium for Houston with a sliding roof in case of rain … Most imposing of all is McCarthy's showy and opulent new Shamrock Hotel. In causing its white, glass-tiered, palm-bordered bulk to rise above the Texas coastal plain, McCarthy endowed Houston with the Southwest's most luxurious hostelry—a soft-carpeted, $21 million palace which boasts French cooking [filet mignon: $11], air-conditioned bedrooms with both push-button radio and Muzak, afternoon tea served to string music and big-name dinner entertainers like Edgar Bergen and Dorothy Lamour … Glenn McCarthy is as peculiarly a product of Texas as the famed San Jacinto monument; the Lone Star State is one of the few places left in the world where millionaires hatch seasonally, like May flies.

> *Bryan Burrough paints a comprehensive and colorful picture of oil-boom Texas with his* The Big Rich: The Rise and Fall of the Greatest Texas Oil Fortunes, *weaving together the stories of Hugh Roy Cullen, Sid Richardson, H.L. Hunt and Clint Murchison.*

KENNEDY SLAIN
ON DALLAS STREET

GRAY CLOUDS WENT AWAY
Day Began as Auspiciously As Any in Kennedy's Career

[*Robert E. Baskin, chief of the Washington Bureau of The News, was one of four persons representing the world press in the motorcade which resulted in the President's assasination. This is his account of what happened.*]

It was a day that started as auspiciously as any in the career of John F. Kennedy. When we boarded the Presidential jetliner, Air Force One, at Forth Worth at midmorning, the White House party was in high spirits. The Fort Worth welcome has been a tremendous one. Shortly before the 15-minute flight to Love Field, ugly gray clouds were swept away by a brisk breeze. The sun was out, and the Texas sky was a vivid blue. President and Mrs. Kennedy, she strikingly attired in a pink suit with a pert matching hat, made an instant hit at Love Field as they shook hands with hundreds of persons along the fence line. The the last journey began. The big open Lincoln car moved out smoothly, carrying Mr. and Mrs. Kennedy and Gov. John Connally and his wife, Nellie. Three cars back was the press pool car, in which three other newspapermen and I rode. Just ahead of us was Dallas Mayor and Mrs. Earle Cabell and Rep. Ray Roberts of McKinney. Malcolm Kiulduff, assistant press secretary, was with us, and as we moved into the heart of the city Kilduff expressed elation over the friendly nature of the welcome and the great outpouring of people. Everyone in the press car agreed it was one of the most cordial receptions President has received in quite a while. Buoyed by the cheers of the multitudes on Main Street, our motorcade moved on past the courthouse. Then came the approach to the Triple Underpass, with the leading cars picking us speed as the crowd thinned out. Over to the right loomed the gaunt structure labeled the Texas

State School Book Depositary. It was 12:30 p.m. The sharp crack of a rifle rang out. But at that moment we couldn't believe it was just that. "What the hell was that?" someone in our car asked. Then there were two more shots—measured carefully. We saw people along the street diving for the ground. Several persons shielded children. Then we knew that the presidential party was under fire. The motorcade ground to a halt. There was a good bit of activity around the President's car, however, police sirens began wailing loudly. The President's car started up and quickly was going at breakneck speed. We did well to keep up with it, skidding around corners. At that point we did not know what had happened—whether the President was merely being rushed out of the danger zone or if someone has been hit by a shot. We began to suspect the worst when we roared up to the emergency entrance of Parkland Hospital. The scene there was one of sheer horror. The President lay face down on the back seat of the car, with Mrs. Kennedy her hair disheveled and her hat gone, slumped over him.

The bouquet of roses she had been carrying was on top of the President. There was blood on the flor. In the seat in front of them, Nelly Connally was holding her husband. The door was opened and Connally, with assistance, stood up momentarily beside the car. A large patch of blood showed on his right shoulder. Connally sighed deeply. He was placedon a mobile stretcher immediately. The policemen lifted Kennedy out of the back seat,and he was hurriedly wheeled away on another stretcher. A little ater two priests appeared at the hospital. When they came out of the President's room, they said the last rites of the church had been administered, but they did not indicate that he was dead. The word came later. President Kennedy died at about 1 p.m. Outside the sun was still shining, but the day seemed to have been transformed completely as the horror of this day—almost unbelievable—began to sink in on us for the first time.

Robert E. Baskin for
The Dallas Morning News,
Saturday, November 23, 1963

BUM STEERS

Texas Monthly's Bum Steer Awards are legendary. Intended to bestow comic appreciation to the worst among us, winners have ranged from Governor Dolph Briscoe to Wanda Holloway. The #1 Bums:

1974* .... Dolph Briscoe
1975* .... UT Regents
1976* .... Dolph Briscoe
1977* .... Dolph Briscoe, Madalyn Murray O'Hair
1978* .... Jimmy Carter, Farrah Fawcett
1979 ..... 60,000 UT fans singing "Happy Birthday" to Bevo
1980..... The '70s
1981 ..... The mania over J.R. Ewing
1982 ..... Mike Martin
1983...... Jackie Sherrill
1984...... Carolyn Farb
1985 ..... George H.W. Bush
1986 ..... James Michener
1987 ..... Texas USA, official sesquicentennial bull
1988 ..... Bill Clements
1989 ..... H.R. "Bum" Bright
1990 ..... Exxon
1991...... Clayton Williams
1992 ..... Wanda Holloway
1993...... George H.W. Bush, Ross Perot
1994..... Ross Perot
1995 ..... Texas Democrats
1996 ..... Anna Nicole Smith

1997 ..... Michael Irvin
1998 ..... Drew Nixon
1999 ..... Barney, Ken Starr
2000 .... Matthew McConaughey
2001..... George W. Bush
2002..... Anna Nicole Smith
2003..... Anna Nicole Smith
2004 .... Tom DeLay, Rick Perry, David Dewhurst, Tom Craddick
2005..... Jessica Simpson
2006..... Harriet Miers
2007..... Dick Cheney
2008..... Dennis Franchione
2009..... Roger Clemens
2010 ..... Tom DeLay
2011...... Dallas Cowboys, Texas Longhorns
2012 ..... Rick Perry
2013...... Lance Armstrong
2014..... Houston Astros, Houston Texans, David Dewhurst
2015 ..... Wendy Davis
2016 ..... Blue Bell
2017 ..... Trump Fever
2018 ..... Dan Patrick
2019 ..... Alex Jones
2020..... Beto O'Rourke, Dennis Bonnen

*No clear winner, but one thing is clear: Briscoe sure left his mark

BE A PEPPER

Pharmacist Charles Alderton first introduced patrons at Morrison's Old Corner Drug Store to his "Waco" soda pop formulation. In 1885, the drink made its commercial debut with the name Dr. Pepper. A 1907 ad boasts.

EVERYBODY DRINKS
Dr Pepper
The Pure Food Drink

WHY?
For Many Reasons:

1st.   Because it is so Pure.

2nd.   Because it is so Heathful.

3rd.   Because it is so Palatable and Pleasing to the Taste.

4th.   Because it is so Refreshing.

5th.   Because nothing quenches the thirst so well.

6th.   Because you can get it at all fountains for five cents.

7th.   Because it is Registered under the Pure Food and Drugs Act of June 30th, 1906. Serial number 1965.

8th.   Because It Leaves a Pleasant Farewell— A Gracious Call Back.

ALL FOUNTAINS
5¢

WHATABURGER

Harmon Dobson and Paul Burton co-founded the burger chain in 1950. Whataburger's ["What A Burger!"] first location, on Ayers Street in Corpus Christi, looked similar to many low slung joints of the day. But in 1961, along the dusty plains of Odessa, Dobson [Burton split in '51] debuted the first of the company's now-iconic A-frame buildings. The striking, vertical shape, accented with "International Orange" stripes, was meant to draw attention far and wide. Ads in *The Odessa American*—"Andrews Highway at 37th, West Texas' Finest Taste Treat"—ran alongside a sketch of the "family drive-inn."

SPINDLETOP

"Oil Struck Near Beaumont"
A Stream of Petroleum Shot Into the Air for a Hundred Feet.
Houston Daily Post
January 11, 1901

Beaumont, Texas, January 10—Beaumont is excited tonight and it has good reason to be. About three miles south of the city there is spouting an oil well the equal of which can not be seen elsewhere in the United States and probably in the world. Captain A.F. Lucas, a geologist of Washington, D.C., made the lucky strike. The captain has been prospecting in the vicinity of Beaumont for more than two years. He has spent thousands of dollars with indifferent results until this morning, when the inside pipe in a hole in which he was operating blew high into the air, and it was followed by a six-inch stream of oil, which spouts nearly fifty feet higher than the sixty foot derrick ... The correspondent visited Captain Lucas this afternoon, but that gentleman was so happy over his strike that he would not talk. He merely hugged the reporter and pointing to the oil as it sailed high into the air, said: 'Its equal can not be seen on earth!' Under existing conditions there is no way of estimating the flow of oil, but Captain Lucas says 5000 barrels per day would be exceedingly low.

CELEBRATED GUSHERS

1866
MELROSE
Nacogdoches County
First oil-producing [10 barrels]
drilled well

....

1930
JOINER DAISY BRADFORD NO. 3
Henderson
Biggest East Texas find;
regulation followed

1923
SANTA RITA NO. 1
Big Lake
Permian Basin
breakthrough

....

1998
S. H. GRIFFIN NO. 4
Ponder
Mitchell Energy drills; fracking
boom kickoff

COTTON BOWL CLASSIC
9:03 P.M. TEXAS TIME—JAN. 1, 1964
FROM THE LBJ RANCH, NEAR STONEWALL, TEXAS

> *The President and Lady Bird call Darrell and Edith Royal to congratulate UT on its win over Navy in the Cotton Bowl; discuss Lynda Johnson's attendance at Cotton Bowl; Ludwig Erhard's [West Germany's Chancellor] visit to Hill Country.*

DARRELL ROYAL: Thank you, Mr. President, that's mighty nice of you to call. Gee this, this is a real honor.

LYNDON BAINES JOHNSON: Well, it's a real honor to have you as a citizen our state, my friend. You've brought it more glory and reflected greater credit than just nearly anything I know of that's happened.

DR: Well, thank you, sir.

LBJ: And I hope you'll tell that sweet wife of yours how proud Lady Bird and I are of both of you and I know that she's entitled to about 60 percent of the credit.

DR: [*laughing*] You're exactly right. She's standing right here with me.

LBJ: Well, let me talk to her.

DR: Alright, sir.

LBJ: [*Tell Lady Bird to come on in*]

EDITH ROYAL: Hello, how are ya?

LBJ: Hi, sweetie. I told him to tell you I knew that you were entitled to about 60 percent of the credit.

ER: [*laughing*] Well, that's mighty sweet ,but I tell ya, I didn't sweat a drop today.

LBJ: Well, it was, it was a beautiful thing. I was just talking to Senator [Richard] Russell up in Georgia, and he said that he just never had seen a job done better, won better executed.

ER: Well, I hope you were able to relax and watch a little while.

LBJ: Well, I did, for a little while and it got kinda uninteresting after you got so many touchdowns up there. I, I like to needle all these Texas people that I'm around. You know I got a wife, and a daughter and all of em.

ER: My children sat up by Lynda today. My 11-year-old son was so fascinated with being able to sit up there with the Secret Service men that he was just beside himself.

LBJ: [*laughs*] Well, bless his heart, bless his heart. Lady Bird wants to say hidy to you, honey.

ER: Good.

LADY BIRD JOHNSON: Mrs. Royal?

ER: Hello, how are you?

LADY BIRD: Well, my earnest and happy congratulations to you and your husband.

ER: Thank you. We are so honored that y'all would take time to call us. I've been—I tried to get you to say a word to you the other day.

LADY BIRD: I can't fib but what I had a tiny little bit of a divided heart [*laughing*].

ER: Yes, and I'm sure it was hard on Lynda sittin' up there.

LADY BIRD: Actually! You know, I thought it would be, but she said, "Mama, those Yankees keep on talking about we're really not a terribly good team. We're playing a low conference, whether you don't have to fight hard and now they're gonna' have to realize we do have to fight hard." And so Lynda Bird, wasn't, she wasn't, she wasn't as disturbed as I thought she would be.

ER: Well good. That's real, that's real good. You give her a great big hug and kiss for saying that for me.

LADY BIRD: I will.

ER: So good to talk to you.

LADY BIRD: And my happy happy congratulations to your wonderful husband. And here's Lyndon.

ER: OK.

LBJ: Honey, is Darrell there? Let me talk to him and good luck to you.

ER: Thank you.

DR: Hello.

LBJ: Enjoyed you coming out the other day and tell all your boys I'm mighty proud of each one of 'em.

DR: Well, Mr. President I'm gonna be talking—I'm sure that they'll ask me to say something in just a minute and with your permission I'd like to tell 'em...

LBJ: You just tell 'em that they reflected great glory and great pride in our state and we are all so proud of their fine patriotism and manhood and sportsmanship and we know that they spent a lot of hours tryin' to—that was reflected there today. And we just, our buttons are bustin'.

DR: Well, thank you so much

LBJ: You just, you just say, you quote me, anything you quote me, I'll testify I said it.

DR: [*laughs*] All right then. I also want to thank you for the kind invitation to come over to Stonewall.

LBJ: Well, we enjoyed havin' you. Wasn't that a wonderful thing?

DR: It was a thrill.

LBJ: I've been reading all the German press on it tonight and the German people just went wild about it.

DR: Did they? Well, wonderful.

LBJ: The chancellor went back and told 'em all it happened and they were so proud of their, their people that come over here in 1840 and so forth.

DR: Well, that's great.

LBJ: Well, I'll be seeing you Darrell, and good luck to you, and you're entitled to some rest now and get it. Tell all your boys hello for me.

DR: I certainly will.

LBJ: Bye.

DR: Goodnight.

Telephone conversation #1131, LBJ Presidential Library

LIFE OF QUANAH PARKER, COMANCHE CHIEF

By His Son, Chief Baldwin Parker

The Comanches swarmed like hornets, forming a wide circle so as to close entirely about the white men ... Then the unexpected happened. Over a hill dashed Lieut. Boehm followed by forty Tonkoway Indian scouts and white soldiers, and back of them raced five hundred soldiers of the Fourth Cavalry led by General Mackenzie. Quanah turned and fled. The Comanches trailed after him, but Lieut. Boehm and his scouts kept on without stopping. They reached the place where the brave little group had made such a splendid fight, and Boehm, without drawing rein, shouted, "Bob, you take the left; I'll take the right of the line. Push 'em now. Mackenzie is right in our rear!" The horse on which Lieut. Carter was riding had reached its last atom of strength, and as it fell, exhausted, the young officer was crushed against a huge rock ... And Quanah, chief of the Quahada's, through strategy never excelled by an Indian leader, managed to elude the troops of the Fourth and the Tenth, and wandered out on the edge of the terrible desert which was known as the Staked Plains of Texas: a place where white men died for lack of water, but which the Comanches under Quanah did not hesitate to face.

Baldwin Parker Narrative, 1930, Dolph Briscoe Center for American History, The University of Texas at Austin

OBITS

STEVIE RAY VAUGHAN   August 27, 1990

"That boy came from nowhere, and he went everywhere. He was the consummate Texas blues artist." *The Dallas Morning News*

SELENA QUINTANILLA   March 31, 1995

"She was starting to bloom not only as an artist but as a person ... Tejano music is dead for at least today." *Corpus Christi Caller-Times*

DJ SCREW   November 16, 2000

"It just kind of vibrates through your soul...Just think of what could have happened to rap music if he lived." *The New York Times*

BOOT MAKER LEXICON

*In a state home to names like Lucchese, Lama and Little,
boots are high art, and their makers, artists.*

TOE BOX	Inside around toe; can be round, square, steel-toe
THE UPPER	Top of boot, the shaft
SCALLOP	V-shaped dip on the shaft
VAMP	Boot's lower front end
WING-TIP	Leather piece [high-end] affixed to toe
ROPER	Style with a lower heel, shorter shaft
SAINT CRISPIN	Patron saint of boot makers
PULL STRAPS	Straps required to pull on footwear
EARS	Elongated pull straps
PULL HOLES	Finger holes to replace pull straps, also called "windows"
HAND	Softness or fullness of a hide

DANCE HALLS

VENUE	CITY	FOUNDED
Broken Spoke	Austin	1964
Gruene Hall	New Braunfels	1878
Albert Ice House	Stonewall	1922
Luckenbach Hall	Luckenbach	1887
Cadillac Dance Hall	Marble Falls	2007
Hye Dance Hall	Hye	c. 1909
Twin Sisters Dance Hall	Blanco	1870
Kendalia Halle	Kendalia	1903
Billy Bob's Texas	Fort Worth	1981
John T. Floore's	Helotes	1942
London Dance Hall	London	"one of the oldest"

THE GREAT STORM

On September 8, 1900, the deadliest hurricane in U.S. history hit Galveston.

But my dear Mother you got off very easily for most people haven't got a roof to cover them nor a thing to wear. After the water subsided we saw people go by with nothing on but a blanket or a grain sack ... and the deaths—under every fallen house lay the people owning it. We hear horrors every hour too awful to think on. I had to keep my eyes turned from many a sight. People went by homeless and hungry. We went in to see the Porters and found their house off the piles on the ground full of mud and plaster two inches thick ... Why even the jetties are almost gone and the strongest houses ruined. Will end this sorrowful tale and have Mr. H mail it when he goes in tomorrow. With a heart full of love and hoping soon to hear of your plans.

Lovingly,
Sarah

Excerpted from *Through a Night of Horrors: Voices From the* 1900 *Galveston Storm*

BIGGER IN TEXAS

KING RANCH

Its 825,000 acres touch six counties, the running W brand touches 35,000 head of cattle.

BUC-EE'S

Gas station? The New Braunfels spot has 18 acres, 120 pumps. Best bathrooms on I-10, too.

ASTRODOME

The 1965 dome inspired artificial turf [aka AstroTurf], but dilapidation later cost them the Oilers.

BIG TEXAN

The billboard dare: Eat 72-ounce steak, shrimp cocktail, potato, salad, roll. Free if eaten in one hour.

LAKEWOOD CHURCH

Joel Osteen megachurch holds 16,800 Sunday-goers in former Rockets Summit arena.

STATE FAIR

For 24 days, over 2 million visitors down 600,000 "corny dogs," which debuted here in late '30s.

OAKS

Despite pecan holding state tree status, live oaks bear particular importance for Texans, their sprawling branches bearing witness to centuries of toil and triumph. Thanks to years of acorn collecting by the Lady Bird Johnson Wildflower Center, you can visit descendants of the state's historic oaks at the Texas Arboretum in Austin. A look at how these giants gained infamy.

RANGER OAK *Seguin* —Campsite and marker for Gonzales Rangers, forebear to Texas Rangers

PANNA MARIA OAK *Panna Maria* —Site of 1854 Christmas Eve service for some 700-plus weary Polish settlers

CABINET OAK *Stonewall*—LBJ's favorite meeting spot while in residence at the Texas White House

HEART O' TEXAS OAK *Mercury*—Geographic center of state; privately owned but viewable from Ranch Road 1028

KISSING OAK *San Marcos*—Sam Houston pecked state flag-presenting women after campaign speech

TURNER OAK *Fort Worth*—Charles Turner buried gold here during Civil War, retrieved postwar to aid in town's flourishing

---

MARY KAY

In 1963, Mary Kay Ash committed her $5,000 life savings toward starting her namesake cosmetics company with the hope of giving other women the empowerment she had found in direct sales as a single mother. The multilevel marketing company started with nine consultants and in 2015 listed its worldwide count at 3.5 million.

5............... Number of pink Cadillacs awarded to top sellers in 1969
200.......... Consultants at first seminar; ; Ash cooked chicken, cornbread
13............. Floors in The Mary Kay Building; Ash's lucky number
1973 .... Year consultants' uniform was a red dress with cape
83 .... Ash's age when she passed away, in 2001
500.......... Amount paid to tanner J.W. Heath for original formulas

TEXAS RANGERS

1823 .... Founded by Stephen F. Austin, to defend colony against raids

1823 .... First Ranger killed in line of duty, John Jackson Tumlinson Sr.

1835 .... Officially sanctioned by lawmakers; tasked with "ranging and guarding the frontier"

1837 .... Skirmish with the Kichai tribe; 10 members killed

1841 .... Force increased by Sam Houston from 56 to 150 men

1846 .... Assist U.S. troops in the Battle of Monterrey

1858 .... With the Texas Militia, defeat the Comanche in the Battle of Little Robe Creek

1861 .... Texas secedes; many Rangers sign up to fight for the Confederacy

1874 .... First permanent force approved by the Texas Legislature

1874 .... Capture prolific murderer John Wesley Hardin in Pensacola, Florida

1877 .... Surrender in the Salinero Revolt, the Rangers' only such action

1878 .... Take down bank, train and stagecoach robber Sam Bass

1909 .... Prevent the joint assassination of U.S. and Mexican presidents

1918 .... Murder 15 Mexican men and boys in the Porvenir Massacre

1919 .... Canales Investigation reveals abuse of authority, target Mexican and Tejano killings

1933 .... Discharged of duties by governor Ma Ferguson

.... "The Lone Ranger" radio program premieres, feeding the Ranger myth

1935 .... Merge with Highway Patrol to form Texas Department of Public Safety

1960 .... Irene Garza murdered; priest John Feit suspected, trail goes cold

2002 .... Ranger Rudy Jaramillo reopens case; in 2017 85-year-old Feit convicted, sentenced to life

LETTER FROM A RANGER

May 10, 1989

Dear Mr. Duvall,

From the time "Lonesome Dove" filming began, I guess you could say I was skeptical. For I to know, as apparently you do, the difference in a "man's garment" and his "trappings". Especially if it's got some real "age on it". They say an actor has to portray a character 'cause he's only acting out a part. What makes some actors stand out? I say it's being a real professional. Knowing what's on the "inside of a man" is sometimes much more important than what you see on the outside. Of course every film that is successful is the culmination of many things, and I'm aware that it is a cohesive effort on the part of many. However Robert Duvall's "Gus" and Tommy Lee Jones "Woodrow" depiction of "our kind" was "superb" and "without peer". Believe me, I know. Twenty years will make you knowledgeable. Upon viewing of this film, I could see it in your talk, your walk, your facial expression, and your hand jestures. For this, you are to be highly commended ... I lost a fine Ranger friend in a gun battle which ensued over the kidnapping of a little girl about two years back. I thought of him in the film when you both were in the saloon in San Antonio, Texas. You see, real men and Rangers are sometimes temporarily forgotten, and they do have their favorite places, and yes, they do cry at times ... You're the best. Take it from all of us who know and have seen the real McCoy. May God grant you a long life and much happiness and success. "By Gum, it's been quite a party, ain't it?"

Respectfully,

Ron Stewart
Texas Ranger

CABEZA DE VACA

The Spanish explorer was the first nonnative to step foot in Texas. From 1528 to 1536, he and three fellow shipwreck survivors forged their way from Galveston to the Chinati Mountains. Below, an excerpt from his 1542 narrative, La Relación, in which he recalls time spent with the Arbadaos people of far South Texas.

In the entire day we ate nothing more than two fistfuls of that fruit [mesquite], which was green; it had so much milk that it burned our mouths. And there being a lack of water, it produced great thirst in whomever ate it … I have already said how, throughout this entire land, we went about naked, and since we were not accustomed to it, like serpents we changed our skins twice a year. And with the sun and wind, there appeared on our chests and backs some very great ulcerations, which caused us very great distress on account of the large loads we covered, which were very heavy and caused the ropes to cut into the flesh of our arms. And the land is so rugged and impassable that many times when we gathered firewood in the dense thickets, when we finished taking it out we were bleeding in many places from the thorns and brambles that we encountered.

THE REVOLUTION

War raged in Texas with a band of rebels fighting for independence against a Mexican army more than double their size.

The massacre of Col. Fannin's command is confirmed by a letter received by a citizen of this place from his son, who was one of the seven men that escaped from the cold-blooded butchery by the Mexicans of their prisoners of war. Young Shane, the person alluded to above, after incredible fatigues and hardships, reached Houston's camp barefooted, and nearly starved. He states that about 500 persons were shot—a part of whom were Fannin's men: the rest had been captured on other occasions. After being kept without provisions several days, they were marched about half a mile from the Mexican camp, under pretence of giving them something to eat; when, at a signal from the commanding officer of the escort, the work of death commenced; and none but Shane and his companions are now left to tell the fate of their comrades. —*Louisville Advertiser*, 1836

THE BRAZOS

An excerpt from John Graves'
landmark Goodbye to a River.

The shores flattened. In the Hittson and Village Bends the valley of the river's ancient scooping widens for a stretch before the sandstone mountains close in again tightly for a few miles of farewell ... On the river the wind wasn't strong, but high up it was doing violence. The El Greco clouds suddenly, as though consciously, coalesced into a gray overcast that turned the day ominous. Two long skeins of big birds flapped across the grayness toward the south—sand-hill cranes, grating out their castle-gate croak—and I knew what the air's muggy edge meant. Geese confirmed it, the first I'd seen, four snows in a little disciplined V, winging solemnly and soundlessly south. The wind on the river died, and paddling I began to sweat. It was the kind of day that usually, in the Texas fall, is full of a kind of waiting; things are moving, the year is changing, a norther is coming ....

THE UVALDE NEWS
MAY 10, 1940

"Spring In The Brush Country"

In the brush country the coming
 of Spring
Is a fragrant, brazen, beautiful
 thing.
A gorgeous hussy in gaudy attire
Flaunting her favors for all to
 admire.
Indian fire wheels whirl flame
 on the grass
Buttercups proffer you gold—as
 you pass.
Haughty rose thistles—so slender
 and trim—
Sway over daisies—demure and
 prim.
Wine cups hold nectar of fresh
 morning dew—
Lush green mesquite veils the
 heavenly blue;
Tall Spanish daggers lift gleam-
 ing white spears
The sentinel constant—throughout the years.
Spangled and jeweled in soft silver lace.
A spider's web swings with dew
 on its face.
Vain is the painter's brush—
 vain are the pens
To capture this glory where nature transcends.

   —Kitty Ward Stuart

J. FRANK DOBIE

Born in 1888 to a ranching family in Live Oak County, Dobie was a writer and naturalist committed to recording the traditions and attitudes of rural Texans. He is the author of scores of books [Tales of Old-Time Texas, Rattlesnakes] *and maintained a weekly newspaper column from 1939 up to his death, in 1964. His archive, housed at Texas State University's Wittliff Collections, is a treasure trove of correspondence.*

ON RATTLESNAKES

Mr. J Frank Dobie, Austin, Texas.

Dear Sir:—
    After reading your interesting story in the Dallas News several weeks about Rattlesnakes it occurred to me to ask you if you are informed as to whether or not it is unusual for rattlesnakes to have more than one or sometimes two sets or pairs of fangs. I killed a large snake in my front yard this summer and out of curiosity took his fangs out and to my surprise found that it had more than a dozen fangs of varying sizes. If this is unusual or strange and of interest to you I will be glad to send you these fangs.

Yours truly, HH Ratchford Sept. 8th. 1931

BIRDS OF THE CHISOS

Dear Dobie:
    I had an argument with a real cowboy around a campfire in the Chisos Mountains last week about the call of a Stephen's Poor Will. We kept hearing it, and he said it was a Whip Poor Will, and I tried to teach him the distinction between the Poor Will's call and the Whip Poor Will's. I finally made him recognize it, and he saw that I was right. He got out very neatly:
    "Well," concluded he, "I knowed all the time it wasn't exactly the Whip Poor Will's call, but I thought, being down here so fer on the border, he was tryin' to say it in Mexican."
    You can't beat 'em.

"Bedi" [Roy Bedichek, Dobie's lifelong friend], 1936

Dear Mr. Dobie,

One day while my wife and I were driving down a dirt road we saw a Paisano running ahead of us picking up something and swinging it over his head to throw it several feet ahead of him. Each time it struck he was there to throw it again. We discovered this was a rattlesnake ... He took the snake and ran away into the brush. When one of my brother's was a young lad up on the Cibolo, he killed one and asked our mother to clean and fry it. We thought it would be like prairie chicken. When she cut into it she found a foot-long garter snake. I will say there was no Paisano for dinner that day.

One of your readers,
E.L. Patton
1959

CORONADO'S CHILDREN

An excerpt from the introduction to Dobie's Corondao's Children, *published in* 1930.

"In the Beginning"

These tales are not creations of mine. They belong to the soil and to the people of the soil. Like all things that *belong,* they have their roots deep in the place of their being, deep too in the past. They are an outgrowth; they embody the geniuses of divergent races and peoples who even while fiercely opposing each other blended their traditions. However all this may be, the tales are just tales. As tales I have listened to them in camps under stars and on ranch galleries out in the brush. As tales, without any ethnological palaver, I have tried to set them down. So it is with something of an apology that I make even a brief explanation before plunging into a veritable Iliad of adventures.

INCLUDING

064	*The Texas Odyssey*
076	*A Listening Tour*
082	*State of the Arts*
088	*The Border*
092	*East Texas*

ROAD TRIPS

Soulful experiences that take
travelers deep into the
heart of Texas

THE TEXAS ODYSSEY
14-DAY

Here starts the Texas ramble, from briny coastal byways, to wildflowered hill towns, to the far west reaches. The wide-open space is, as Ray Benson sings, "miles and miles of Texas, all the stars up in the sky." From east to west, this is a frontier of well-loved talismans—rodeo buckle, spring-fed city pool, desert canyon—alongside new icons expanding the Texas universe. It's all here. Set forth.

—————

1. HOUSTON 2. GALVESTON 3. ROCKPORT/ARANSAS BAY
4. SAN ANTONIO 5. ROUND TOP 6. AUSTIN
7-8. HILL COUNTRY 9. DALLAS 10. PALO DURO CANYON
11-13. WEST TEXAS 14. BIG BEND NATIONAL PARK

| DAY |
| 1 |

HOUSTON

Explore the city's abundant pockets of international food, containing everything from bánh mì to barbacoa.

Houston's restaurant landscape reflects its status as the most diverse city in the United States. Make your way down Bellaire Boulevard through Asiatown, a nearly 30-mile stretch of restaurant-filled strip malls, to Hong Kong City Mall and follow the scent of oven-fresh bread to ALPHA BAKERY & DELI for a smoky-sweet barbecue pork bánh mì dressed with crunchy carrots and cucumbers, mayo and butter. Sugar-boost with alfajores, a South American sandwich cookie with creamy dulce de leche between crumbly powder-sugared shortbread, at SWEETS BY BELEN or gourmet grocer PHOENICIA SPECIALTY FOODS. Don't overlook the lunch plate specials [cafeteria trays loaded with combos like biryani, paneer curry, garlic naan and chana masala] at Indian-Pakistani staple HIMALAYA RESTAURANT. In Montrose, MALA SICHUAN BISTRO's chef Jianyun Ye earned a James Beard nomination for his mouth-numbing red oil wontons and tea-smoked, three-pepper beaten duck. Nearby, Hugo Ortega's celebrated flagship, HUGO'S, serves Oaxacan classics with housemade queso fresco and an intensely rich, 25-ingredient mole. Bring home traditional Hispanic ingredients, from jars of huitlacoche to dried pasilla chiles, at the HOUSTON FARMERS MARKET on Airline's sprawling stalls brimming with produce and fragrant spices. Finally, don't leave the city limits without indulging in splurge-worthy Japanese tapas and nigiri topped with fish flown in fresh from Japan almost daily at KATA ROBATA. Put your trust in chef Manabu "Hori" Horiuchi's omakase [tasting menu] selections.

"Houston's big. Houston is spread out. But that's what makes it great. There are so many different pockets of the city with delicious food that you'd never find if you didn't explore a little. We celebrate our diversity through food. I opened Underbelly and then UB Preserv to tell the story of Houston food, but it's definitely not just me. You'll see Indian and Vietnamese influences on the menu at Kata Robata, and the turkey necks at Crawfish & Noodles have an incredible combination of flavors from Vietnam and Louisiana. I love living here. I love eating here. Don't underestimate Houston."
—Chris Shepherd, *chef*

DAY 2

GALVESTON

Established in 1836, the port town is filled with golden-era mansions. A walking tour for the architecturally inclined.

1838 MICHAEL B. MENARD HOME

Galveston's oldest building with construction starting in 1837; built for Menard's second wife Catherine Maxwell. Look for annual ticketed events or schedule prearranged tour [20 or more]. *1605 33rd St*

CARR MANSION

Greek Revival mansion built in 1866, now a thoughtfully designed, newly reopened B&B. *1103 33rd St*

MOODY MANSION

Red-brick and limestone marvel once home to powerful Texas cotton mogul William Lewis Moody Jr. *2618 Broadway Ave*

THE BRYAN MUSEUM

Formerly the Galveston Orphans Home, now houses frontier collection: Spanish mother-of-pearl chests, Tom Lea sketches, prisoner-made spurs. *1315 21st St*

1892 BISHOP'S PALACE

Four-story, castle-like Victorian marvel; vermilion turrets, amber exterior, stained-glass windows throughout. *1402 Broadway Ave*

ROCKPORT & ARANSAS BAY

South Texas fishing guide JT Van Zandt shares
thoughts on backwater beauty and personal
transcendence via the fly rod.

"Growing up in Houston, we spent lots of weekends in Galveston, but I don't think I really saw the Texas coast. It's not an obvious beauty. But once you really dig into it, the place shows itself. Year-round, 200 days, I launch my poling skiff, mostly at Goose Island State Park, and move through these waters. Sometimes 20 miles in a day. The fly rod has become a tool for me. It's a way to test the health of a place. Fly-fishing came later for me. I was in college in Austin and I had a bad wreck on a BMX bike, broke my leg like an oak branch. While I was hobbling around on crunches, I wandered into an old fly shop called the Austin Angler. Fishing changed my life almost immediately. The open air, the woods, the water: A calm comes over me when I'm fishing. In retrospect, coming from a broken household, watching my dad [songwriter Townes Van Zandt] slowly go, fly-fishing helped make sense of the world for me. We're so separated from the frontier. But down here, in Rockport and these waters, you see the world. It's the birds first. Pelicans, egrets, whooping cranes and stilts, and on and on. There are thousands of acres of ankle-deep water, with turtle grass, wigeon and spartina, the banks just popping with sounds. Mullet, blue crabs and stone crabs, mud shrimp. And the redfish we're stalking are just partying on all of it. All these creatures, it's spectacular. And it's fragile. Even a baby could be dazzled by it. Everyone who goes out onto these waters just takes a deep breath. I think about how my dad left me his poetry and songs, sort of like a guide. And it reminds me that we all share in this place, this world. I'm far from perfect, but I'm trying to think of others when I'm out here and trying to not do the needless things. How I use the water, how I fish, every decision, every breath. It's a gift." *jtvanzandt.com*

> *Van Zandt recommends two lodging options in Rockport: the newly restored* R.H. WOOD HOUSE *and the dockside* INN AT FULTON HARBOR.

DAY
4

SAN ANTONIO

River City is overflowing with Mexican tradition,
history and culture, as present here as anywhere
south of the border.

CHARREADA

Along the San Antonio River, near Mission County Park, you'll find
Rancho del Charro, where for 70 years the Asociación de Charros
de San Antonio has been gathering [April-November] to compete
and perform. More akin to pageant than rodeo, the Mexican
American charros [men] and escaramuzas [women] honor the 16th-
century hacienda tradition of gathering to "enjoy family, show off
horses and sell livestock," explains commissioner Irma Iris Duran
de Rodriguez. To visit today is to be welcomed into the fold with
a cold beer, food truck flautas and generations of families whose
community is centered at the arena. *sacharros.org*

CONJUNTO

Mennonite Church, in the heart of King William, seems an unlikely
spot to meet a conjunto legend, yet that is what happens every
Monday at 3:30 p.m. Bene Medina arrives ready to play, thanks to the
Conjunto Heritage Taller, an organization committed to offering
daily accordion and bajo sexto classes [Lorenzo Martinez, Richard
Castillo also teach]. "I played at Night in Old San Antonio for 42
years," Medina says with a smile. "Conjunto music started at polkas
and waltzes and here comes this guy called Valerio Longoria playing
a bolero, and later on Paulino Bernal and the cumbias started, and
then Danzones, and I'm one of the lucky ones that can still play all
that." *conjuntoheritagetaller.com*

In a town with no shortage of Tex-Mex offerings, a new generation is honoring the old. Since 2017, CARNITAS LONJA has
been serving up perfect [traditional] carnitas tacos and tortas.
Closed Monday. 1107 *Roosevelt Ave*, [210] 612-3626

| DAY |
| 5 |

ROUND TOP

The twice-a-year Round Top Antiques Fair has grown into a sprawling reunion, where vendors dot 15 miles of cow pasture-lined Highway 237. The standouts.

EXCESS

These vast tents require just enough digging to make you feel like a bona fide picker. Look for Cubist-esque oil paintings to early 20th-Century nautical lighting.

....

THE COMPOUND

Air-conditioned barns known for Eneby Home's midcentury European furniture and Antiques of Dallas' English chests and sideboards.

....

MARBURGER FARM

Tickets required for these designer-favored alphabetized tents open for only one week. At lunchtime, grab a brisket sandwich from Back Porch BBQ.

"Our best 'first pick' are doors originally from a cotton gin in Devine, Texas."
—PAIGE HULL, THE VINTAGE ROUND TOP COTTAGES

| DAY |
| 6 |

AUSTIN

In the midst of a too-good-to-be-true boom, Austin still manages to be chock-full with swimmers, whose best days are one's where they never dry off.

Start at the granddaddy of them all—BARTON SPRINGS POOL—and join the lap-swimming octogenarians, grass-smoking yogis and downriver dog owners as you cool off in the 68-degree waters. Afterward, make your way to JUICELAND's original Barton Springs Road location for a trademark Wundershowzen. Barely dry, hop in the car and head west outta town to HAMILTON POOL, whose horseshoe cliffs surround blue waters. You'll need advance reservations, but you already knew that. Hike back out and fill up on al pastor at TAQUERIA LA ESCONDIDA, next to the Chevron. End your day at spring-fed DEEP EDDY POOL, where the unattached veer left, with parents and their charges, heading right. Post-laps, walk up the hill to POOL BURGER for a Loyal Forever followed by pitchers upstairs at DEEP EDDY CABARET, the best dive bar in town.

HILL COUNTRY

Settled in the 1800s by German immigrants, this
frontier is laced with limestone bluffs and
sunset-hued grasses. One favored pocket.

WILDSEED FARMS

Fredericksburg—The country's largest wildflower farm set within 200
acres of production fields and walking trails. March begins the blooms
with a *Wizard of Oz*-like expanse of red corn poppies followed by
indigo bluebonnets.

....

TWIN SISTERS DANCE HALL

Blanco—Generations of Texans have gathered at these German-built
halls where a country western band leads the town in a public dance.
Join in the two-step tradition on the first Saturday of each month.

....

JENSCHKE ORCHARDS

U.S. 290—Hill Country peaches are serious business and a family
affair. Reach for varieties like June Prince and Rich Lady at this farm
seven generations of Jenschkes have called home.

....

CAROL HICKS BOLTON ANTIQUITIES

Fredericksburg—Treasure-hunt through 30,000 square feet of ancient
European antiques like Parisian café chairs, church reliquaries and
farmhouse tables.

....

GARRISON BROTHERS

Hye—Among the vineyards, the first sanctioned whiskey distillery in
the state. The bourbons benefit from aging in Texas' brutal summer
heat—taking on deeper color and spicier notes.

....

SOUTHOLD FARM + CELLAR

Fredericksburg—While away an afternoon on a porch swing at this mini-
malist-modern winery hailed for its nuanced blends. Proprietors Carey and
Regan Meador also own Johnson City's pocket-size wine bar The Parlour.

....

WALDEN RETREATS

Johnson City—These 96 acres along the Pedernales River are dotted
with luxe, safari tent-style quarters [with claw foot tubs].

SOUTHHOLD
FARM+CELLAR

WALDEN
retreats

Fredericksburg
CITY LIMITS
· Willkommen

JENSCHKE ORCHARDS

CAROL HICKS
BOLTON ANTIQUITIES

290

GARRISON BROS

Wildseed Farms

Twin Sisters Dance Hall

DALLAS

DAY 9

Lean into the center of urbane Texas and embrace the highfalutin.

First opened in 1907, and in its flagship location since 1914, NEIMAN MARCUS still matters. Book an appointment with personal shopper Elsa Norwood and don't forget to grab a Zodiac popover as you head to the classic's cool-aunt equivalent, FORTY FIVE TEN. The editorial destination is a see-and-be-seen feast for the eyes. One TEI-AN sushi lunch later, make your way to the NASHER SCULPTURE CENTER, whose Renzo Piano-designed galleries and Picasso-filled sculpture garden manage to be an escape from material Dallas. After a quick change and, if you're lucky, a JOANNA CZECH facial, close out at the WINSPEAR OPERA HOUSE, where both the Dallas Opera and Texas Ballet Theater are housed.

> In 1936, on the occasion of Texas' Centennial Celebration, Dallas' FAIR PARK was transformed into an art deco showcase. Of the 50 structures, water features and sculptures built, 26 remain today, all just waiting for a visit. *fairpark.org*

PALO DURO CANYON

DAY 10

Georgia O'Keeffe once called the Texas Panhandle home. Here she recalls a trip to the striated canyon, the country's second-largest.

"I've been in the Canyon all afternoon—I didn't climb—I sat on the top all alone—the first time alone—I didn't want to climb—so wore high-heeled slippers ... and I had to laugh at myself sitting there in those shoes ... thinking how feeble-minded I must be to have to hobble myself before I left home to make myself behave ... The very far wide of it—lavender and pink and red and blue—made dirty in places by millions of little scrubby cedars—never more than ten or twelve feet high ... gnarled and twisted ... scrubby little old things but still live and bravely green ... Shadows very blue—I almost cooked—half-asleep in the sun ... I had a great time by myself—The sunset was a long warm glow—it seems to hate to leave this country."

—*Georgia O'Keeffe to Alfred Stieglitz, October 1916*

DAY 11

MARFA

```
The desert is speckled with roadhouses, dives
and watering holes, but one bar draws new and
old West Texas together.
```

At night, the clearest signage outside the LOST HORSE SALOON reads "Beer" aglow in cherry-red neon. The owner, Ty Mitchell, looks straight out of *High Noon* with a ten-gallon hat and leather eye patch. The old-timers in worn-out Wranglers drinking longnecks you expect in a place like this are here, but so is VJ Mellow Arms projecting vintage footage of Iggy Pop on a king-size bedsheet. In the back, the plywood stage presents a constant parade of folk singer-songwriters, upstart psychedelic garage rock bands and country crooners. In this tiny town where blue-collar and no-collar work the fields and studios separately by day, at night they commingle—dust-coated boots, paint-splattered sneakers and hiking shoes all tapping to the same beat.

DAY 12

WEST TEXAS

```
Some of the state's best lodging lies
in its least-populated portion.
```

BRITE BUILDING

MARFA—An in-town, more conventional outpost of campground cousin El Cosmico, this 3,800-square-foot loft sits above the Ayn Foundation gallery displaying Andy Warhol's "The Last Supper" series. Best for a big crew.

....

WILLOW HOUSE

TERLINGUA—Concrete block casitas resembling a minimalist art piece with uninterrupted views of sunrises over the Chisos and Milky Way-plastered skies at night. Inside, the amenities belie the property's Spartan appearance.

....

GAGE HOTEL

MARATHON—Originally built as guest quarters by a prominent rancher in 1927, its rooms come complete with cowhide chairs and leather headboards. Cowboys still conduct business over lowballs at the adjoining White Buffalo Bar.

TERLINGUA

Trace the horizon by horseback where the edges of
a ghost town and Big Bend National Park meet.

A smattering of structures strewn across the foothills beneath the
Chisos Mountains—adobe cottages, a theater, art project hovels,
a subterranean dive bar, generator-run camping trailers, a general
store, a gas station and, more recently, a few yurts—it's hard to
imagine Terlingua was once a globally known quicksilver mining hub
with a few thousand residents. Today, the population officially stands
at 60-ish, but come sunset, it's less difficult to see the reasons why
they call this hardscrabble hamlet home. Head out on horseback
on a guided two-hour ride from BIG BEND STABLES, which takes
you around the town's old mine shaft, through Rough Run Creek
and along the spine of the mountain ridge overlooking the national
park as the sky shifts from golden hour to streaks of indigo, amber,
bougainvillea pink and violet. *lajitasstables.com*

BIG BEND NATIONAL PARK

Venture through one of America's least-visited
national parks and see a different side of the
borderland along the Rio Grande.

A millennia-old landscape with patches of ground no human has ever
walked, Big Bend and its absence of sound and movement fill the soul.
The towering, sienna-colored Chisos Mountains that rickrack the
horizon give way to the lush, jade Rio Grande valley—jawdropping
countryside that lives by its own rules. Drive down a true open road
toward Grapevine Hills Trail [2.2 miles], where an easy hike leads to
Balanced Rock, a geological marvel of suspended boulders perched
over wildflowers. The park is bookended by two sheer canyons, Santa
Elena and Boquillas. The latter leads toward Boquillas del Carmen,
a resilient village on the Mexican side of the border [seasonal hours,
bring your passport for legal entry]. From there, take a three-minute
boat ride into town to shop handicrafts and have a beer at Park Bar.
Close the day with a restoring soak at the Historic Hot Springs, where
the original 1909 structure separated the 105-degree water from the
Rio Grande's much chillier current.

A LISTENING TOUR
5-DAY

Hit these historic venues in a single
week and you'll walk away with a full-
tilt appreciation for dance halls and
roadhouses, as well as the music itself.
All visits accompanied with a side of
barbecue, the meat and potatoes of
Texas cuisine, minus the potatoes. And
know, these are participatory places,
where the audience can be as much
a part of the show as the performers
onstage. Come prepared to be in the
middle of the action.

Written by
JOE NICK PATOSKI

———

1. HOUSTON 2. GOLIAD 3. FISCHER
4. AUSTIN 5. SEATON

HOUSTON
Get into the swing at these neighborhood clubs
harking back to Houston's rich blues history.

THE SILVER SLIPPER sits on Houston's near northeast side in Kashmere Gardens, on the edge of what was once known as Frenchtown for its population of Louisiana Creoles. The joint, run by Dorothy and Curley [son of original owner, Alfred] Cormier, functions as the local bar hangout during most of the week. But on Saturday nights, round about 10 p.m., Curley takes the bandstand with his group, The Gladiators, along with guest vocalists, including featured singer Joe Hill, as they run through soul and R&B classics and standards. The small dance floor in the red-lit room fills, the singers work the tables, and by midnight, the whole joint is buzzing, punctuated by laughs and the occasional scream of pure pleasure—a window into Houston's rich blues past. Versions of Johnnie Taylor's "Wall to Wall" and Tyrone Davis' "Turning Point" are crowd favorites. Upon arrival, head to the bar in back and introduce yourself to Dorothy, who knows all and sees all and likes to take care of first-time visitors. *3717 Crane St*

THE BIG EASY SOCIAL & PLEASURE CLUB is the place in Houston showcasing black roots music. Says blues hound John Branch, "Everyone at some point plays at The Big Easy." And while there's nothing fancy about the brick storefront on the Kirby strip near Rice Village, it's the music made inside that separates the club from all others in H-Town. It feature blues six nights a week and zydeco on Sundays, with jam sessions Wednesdays, the Houston Blues Society jam every last Thursday of the month and the National Zydeco Foundation jam on last Sundays. This is the place to hear Step Rideau and The Zydeco Outlaws and Raa-Raa Zydeco, two of the top bands cranking out the Creole sound popular in Southeast Texas and neighboring Louisiana. The "Social & Pleasure" part of the club's name is a nod to New Orleans, where social and pleasure organizations are numerous. The sparkly décor suggests a permanent party going down. *thebigeasyblues.com*

> **GATLIN'S BBQ** serves up top-shelf brisket,
> pulled pork with classic East Texas soul sides. Beef ribs
> on the weekend. *gatlinsbbq.com*

SCHROEDER HALL, GOLIAD

A remnant of the 19th-century immigrant
community called Germantown, Schroeder Hall
stands the test of time.

Schroeder Hall is the place to hear Texas country music, that weird hybrid of traditional country western and the genre-bending progressive sound that broke out of Texas in the 1970s. Recently upgraded and renovated, the wooden building with the bungalow tin roof is actually the second version of the dance hall, built in 1935 after a fire destroyed the original hall, erected in 1890. The saloon stays busy whether there's music in the hall or not. But when bands are playing expect to see a dance floor filled with two-steppers, waltzers and polkaholics. *schroederhall.com*

> Louis McMillan of MCMILLAN'S BAR-B-Q has been turning out
> 'cue for 45 years, and it shows, particularly the brisket, which is
> slow-smoked with a heady mix of mesquite, oak and pecan.
> 9913 US 59 N, Fannin, [361] 645-2126

DEVIL'S BACKBONE TAVERN, FISCHER

Head west across the Gulf prairie and up into the
Hill Country to experience a real Texas honky-tonk.

Schedule your visit to this iconic roadhouse for Barrelhouse Tuesdays, when folks like Emily Gimble and Eric Hokkanen pack the bar by playing it hot and loose. Acts like Johnny Bush, Gary P. Nunn and Willis Alan Ramsey keep the floor moving in the adjacent dance hall on weekends and evenings. Bonus points for the shuffleboard table. The refined level of musical acts reflects the tastes of owners John "Lunchmeat" and Robyn Ludwick, and Abbey Road. *devilsbackbonetavern.com*

> CREEKSIDE COOKERS BBQ is a brick-and-mortar offspring of the
> trailer that schoolteacher Kelly Evers opened in 2016 before quit-
> ting his day job. 500 River Rd., Wimberley, *creeksidecookers.com*

SAM'S TOWN POINT, AUSTIN

A portal to the Austin of a half-century ago where the beer is cheap, food is served on the side, and some of the smartest bands in town occupy the space that passes for a stage.

Located in the back of a '70s-era subdivision, Sam's is more neighborhood dive than fancy-ass nightclub, per the cheap-ass wood paneling that was put up 30 years ago, the "Friends Are the Best Part of Life" message below the "Exit" sign and the sparkly red Christmas lights strung around the room. No matter if it's Pedal Steel Mondays, when the finest steel guitarists in town show off their skills as featured artists, or the genre-bending accordion shootouts between conjunto ace Josh Baca of Los Texmaniacs and Cajun stylist Jesse Lége, or Saturday nights, when Ramsay Midwood, the droll singer-songwriter who owns the club, steps from behind the bar to perform a set, the music is a sure shot; no ringers work this joint. 2115 *Allred Rd, samstownpointatx.com*

Head even farther south on Menchaca Rd [formerly Manchaca and forever pronounced "Man-shack"] to queue up at VALENTINA'S TEX MEX BBQ, this part of town's version of the Franklin Line. San Antonio native Miguel Vidal, his brother Elias and family have mastered smoked brisket, pork and chicken and can hardly meet demand. Breakfast tacos start at 7:30 a.m., smoked meats until 9 p.m. or sold out. *valentinastexmexbbq.com*

TEXAS PLAYLIST

SIDE A

WAY TO THE SHOW	Solange
TURNING POINT	Tyrone Davis
MILES AND MILES OF TEXAS	Asleep at the Wheel
MUSTANG RIDGE	Tanya Tucker
THAT'S RIGHT [YOU'RE NOT FROM TEXAS]	Lyle Lovett

<table>
</table>

DAY 5	**TOM SEFCIK HALL, SEATON**

Conclude your two-step circuit at a classic hall whose weekend dances are as lively as ever.

Once upon a time, Central Texas was full of places that catered to Czech, German and Moravian immigrants who farmed the surrounding prairie. Many venues were SPJST Lodges, run by local chapters of a Czech fraternal benefit organization. Tom Sefcik Hall was the exception, founded in 1923 as a family-run entertainment enterprise and still in the Sefcik family today. Set in the rich rolling blackland fields east of Temple, Sefcik is the only action for miles around. The two-story white-clapboard exterior may show its age, but the interior, with its centerpiece polished-wood dance floor upstairs bordered by tables and facing an old-fashioned inverted stage and the low-ceilinged bar downstairs, has been lovingly maintained. Sunday dances with polka bands draw area old-timers, with live music and karaoke on weekends. The hall's matron, Alice Sefcik Sulak, Tom's daughter, has retired from running the place but still shows up to play her sax on occasion. 800 *Seaton Rd*

MILLER'S SMOKEHOUSE grew out of Dirk Miller's taxidermy and meat-processing business into the ruling king of 'cue between Waco and Austin, in no small part due to Dirk's son, Dusty, who founded the joint with his dad, runs the day-to-day and moved the business to its new location in Belton. Beer and margaritas. *millerssmokehouse.com*

TEXAS PLAYLIST

SIDE B

TEXAS SUN	Khruangbin w/Leon Bridges
IN HEAVEN THERE IS NO BEER	Flaco Jiménez
CALL OF MY HEART	Toni Price
AFTER YOU'VE GONE	Floyd Domino w/Emily Gimble
THE ROAD GOES ON FOREVER	Joe Ely

STATE OF THE ARTS
5-DAY

In 1892, the first museum in Texas was founded with the intention of bringing a fine and cultured influence to the region's cattle-focused residents. This civilizing desire, combined with a sudden influx of petroleum wealth, led to the establishment of fine-art institutions backed by barons with names like Bass, de Menil and Kimbell. Over the past 30 years, that arts patronage boom has widened to include an east-west trail of artist's studios, contemporary salons and conceptual installations. A feast for the eyes and soul, you'll behold everything from sketched broncos and plains to ultraviolet prisms of light.

———

1. HOUSTON 2. FORT WORTH
3. SAN ANTONIO 4-5. MARFA

<table>
<tr><td>DAY
1</td><td>HOUSTON
From original Rauschenbergs to warehouse
studios, Houston's contemporary art scene
embraces the established and the burgeoning.</td></tr>
</table>

TIME	ACTIVITY
Sunrise	SKYSPACE: James Turrell's "Twilight Epiphany" acts as a theater to behold the changing colors of the sun's rising and setting. First of three.
8 AM	PROJECT ROW HOUSES: Community art space with 39 structures that provide artist studio space and housing for young mothers.
10 AM	HIRAM-BUTLER GALLERY: Stroll through the serene showrooms hung with work by Richard Serra and Ellsworth Kelly. Nice work if you can get it.
12 PM	THE MUSEUM OF FINE ARTS, HOUSTON: The newly built Kinder Building will house the museum's rapidly grow-ing collection, including its renowned photography cata-log. Turrell's "The Light Inside," makes two of three.
3 PM	THE MENIL COLLECTION: A 30,146-square-foot modern art institution sits alongside a Cy Twombly-devoted gallery; take a short walk to the recently renovated Rothko Chapel.
4 PM	ART LEAGUE HOUSTON: The nonprofit brings in surpris-ing exhibitions from oil portraits of domestic workers to botanical renderings of grocery lists.
Sunset	LIVE OAK FRIENDS MEETING HOUSE: Visit this commu-nity of silent worshipers whose meeting house is also home to Turrell's "One Accord." Open every Friday and the first Sunday of each month, 30 minutes before sunset. Three of three.

FORT WORTH

Cowboys and ranchers converge, providing a home for portrayers of the West.

"My father is a Western artist. To me it means showing contemporary ranchers, cowboys and portraying them in an honest light. You know bucking' horses, cattle and thunderstorms, that vastness. I work on ranches, so when I'm out there I'm sketching ideas. I do that spring and fall, and the rest of the year I'm back in the studio. The Amon Carter Museum—they've got one of my favorite Remingtons. ["*Ridden Down*", Frederic Remington] An Indian standing in silhouette—his horse has given out and he's standing there and you can see his war party coming for him. The set up is strange, colors contrasting. It shouldn't work but it just works. It brings the viewer in. The romance of the West isn't just romance. There are a lot of hardships." —*Teal Blake, painter*

The Kimbell Art Museum's sublimely vaulted Louis I. Kahn building houses a collection of 350, ranging from Picasso nudes to Sumerian objects to Goya portraits.

SAN ANTONIO

Thanks to the work of two extraordinary women, along with an active community of artists, San Antonio is a bona fide art-world destination.

THE MCNAY ART MUSEUM

Marion Koogler McNay, art collector and oil heiress, died in 1950, leaving her private art collection [Monet, Cassatt, Rivera] and Sunset Hills estate to San Antonio for the purpose of creating Texas' first modern art museum. The McNay, a Spanish Colonial Revival home, perched on 23 Alamo Heights-adjacent acres, is alluring in its grandeur. And while tempting to focus on McNay's story and setting, at the McNay, the art wins the day. Take your time winding through thematic galleries that bounce from Marsden Hartley to Joan Mitchell to Kehinde Wiley, culminating in the more recent Stieren Center addition, and don't forget to take a peek into McNay's personal library. *mcnayart.org*

RUBY CITY

Linda Pace's devotion to artists was immense. A member of San Antonio's Pace Foods family and an artist herself, she founded artist-in-residence Artpace, in 1993. Pace dreamed of a "red art castle," and while she didn't live to see Ruby City's 2019 opening [Pace died in 2007], the groundwork had already been laid for both the hard-to-believe David Adjaye building and the feminist- and social justice-focused collection it houses. The free museum, with its angular coral sandstone exterior, is all in service of work created, and collected, by Pace: Marina Abramović, Cruz Ortiz and Do Ho Suh, to name a few. A strangely wonderful vermilion art fortress for all. *rubycity.org*

> *"There is an amazing contemporary art scene here and I've found it so accessible—a lot of working artists. Plus, we are a minority-majority city steeped in Mexican culture. My students, they're trying to understand what it means to be Chicano, Latina, Hispanic, Latinx, and I have these conversations in my own work."*
>
> **JENNIFER LING DATCHUK, ARTIST, PROFESSOR, TEXAS STATE SCHOOL OF ART AND DESIGN**

DAYS 4-5

MARFA

While the "art oasis" mystique is not a secret, what captured Donald Judd's imagination remains.

No matter how far Marfa's reputation reaches, the town itself continues to be difficult to grasp, literally and figuratively. It hides an hour off the interstate and hundreds of miles from any major airport. Still, Marfa seduces many to drive across the Chihuahuan Desert, in particular artists who seek refuge to create without noise and the curious culturati who flock to them. Much of what makes Marfa shimmer can be found downtown from shop-gallery WRONG STORE to printer ARBER & SONS EDITIONS and exhibition space BALLROOM MARFA. But the past five years have brought new additions like vintage-art boutique RABA MARFA, powder coat artist CODY BARBER's open studio and locals-endorsed festival MARFA MYTHS [limited to 800 tickets], which has grown into a multiday art and music gathering for DIY makers and musicians.

When Donald Judd moved to Marfa in 1971, the tumbleweed town, on
a downswing from a rail station and military base closure, was home to
mainly ranching families and almost no one else. Lured by how he could see
the contour of the land in the absence of trees, Judd himself shaped much
of the Marfa that would last beyond his 1994 death in ways both seen and
unseen. Below, a short guide to the artist's properties and installations.

PRINT BUILDING

Judd bought this downtown building, formerly a hotel, hoping
to display his collection of prints, but passed away shortly after
purchasing it. It now houses the Judd Foundation's Marfa offices and
archives along with two aluminum sculptures. *juddfoundation.org*

....

LA MANSANA DE CHINATI & THE BLOCK

Tours available daily—In an adobe walled-compound, Judd and his
two children lived in a simple home adjacent to two hangars where
he kept a 13,000-volume library organized by subject along with
many of his works, which are sealed inside. In his will, Judd wished
for his art and the architecture around it to never be separated.

....

THE STUDIOS

Tour available every day except Wednesday—A collection of downtown
buildings [once a bank, barbershop, Safeway market] dotting North
Highland and West Oak Streets, served as Judd's painting galleries,
architecture workshop and furniture design spaces, respectively. He
had attempted to join some of them with a wall and a produce stand.

....

THE CHINATI FOUNDATION

Tour available Wednesday through Sunday—This museum exhibits
Judd's most definitive work, which intrinsically connects art with
the land: "15 Untitled Works in Concrete." Set in a field of tall desert
grass, the series of hollow blocks change in light and shadow as the
sun moves across the open sky. *chinati.org*

The Big Bend Sentinel, West Texas' oldest newspaper, continues
to thrive against all odds, now operating in a design-minded
community space and coffee shop. *209 W El Paso St*

THE BORDER

The 1,254-mile southern corridor, from lush valleys to desert no man's land, might be the most misunderstood place in Texas.

TEMP
84 HIGH, 60 LOW

SUNRISE
7:13 AM

SUNSET
8:02 PM

RAINY DAYS PER MONTH
2

TRIP COST
$1300 FOR 2

SEASONAL ACTIVITIES
BEACH SWIMMING, HIKING, KAYAKING

In recent years, the Texas borderlands have been roiled in social crisis and political jockeying. Headlines fixated on detention center cruelty, drug smuggling, a mythical wall—and rightly so. The region's turmoil is real, the stories dire. But what's also true is that the Texas border, from the Rio Grande Valley through Big Bend into the Sun City of El Paso, is more than what the news portrays. Exploring for yourself, one experiences a coalescence of natural wonders along the river and a vaquero remix in border towns.

DAY
1

BROWNSVILLE

In Brownsville, a trio of taquerias are a delicious window into the norms of life in the Rio Grande Valley.

BREAKFAST

Sylvia's Restaurant 1843 *Southmost Blvd*
Buenas dias with tortillas de harina [breakfast tacos on 10-inch tortillas, filled with ingredients like salted beef and scrambled eggs].

....

LUNCH

Vera's Backyard Bar-B-Que [Fri-Sun] 2404 *Southmost Blvd*
A destination for taco pilgrims and the most trusted spot in town to get traditional pit-cooked barbacoa, made from the head of a calf.

....

DINNER

El Ultimo Taco Taqueria 938 *N Expressway*
Unassuming late-night spot that's a perennial favorite of taco tourists. Order a tray of bistek tacos covered in crumbly white cheese.

RIO GRANDE VALLEY The Lower Rio Grande Valley is a crossroads in the sky, of sorts. If Audubon could circle the map, he'd tell you that this is the southern limit for many Eastern and Western avian species and a northern stopping point for tropical beauties. And in its bona fides as a migratory bird paradise in spring and fall, and you have a birder's equivalent of Shangri-La. "Go out for two or three hours and you can see a hundred species," says Keith Hackland, a guide and innkeeper at the birder-focused Alamo Inn B&B. Though you could spend two weeks seeing all the parks and preserves in the World Birding Center and beyond, the area's highlights can be whittled down to three sites in a one-day tour. Start 10 minutes from the Alamo Inn at the 2,088-acre SANTA ANA NATIONAL WILDLIFE REFUGE, a tropical jungle where more than 400 species can be spotted. "It's a spectacle not experienced anywhere else in the country," says Hackland. Continue to the nearby ESTERO LLANO GRANDE STATE PARK to catch glimpses of spoonbills, storks and the rare red-crowned parrot. Complete your quest at QUINTA MAZATLAN, a historic adobe mansion in McAllen where the strollable grounds host everything from owls to orioles.

THE DEVILS RIVER

"The water is so clear, it's like being in the Caribbean," says guide Charlie Angell. The notorious and unspoiled river flows over limestone formations that look like coral reefs, offering by far the most serious rapids in Texas. Expect specimen boulders and Class III waterfalls. Beware is often the precursor to asking locals about paddling the Devils. Angell leads four-day paddling expeditions [skill required] with overnights on sycamore-forested islands. If that's too big an ask, drive Dolan Creek Road for 20 graveled miles into Devils River State Natural Area, and hike the 1-mile trail to Finnegan Springs. Most of Devils River is hemmed by private land, so this is the easiest way to catch a glimpse. In night falls, you'll see the best stargazing in the state, too. "It can be life-changing for people," Angell says. "It certainly was for me."

<table>
<tr><td>DAY
3</td><td>

RIVER ROAD

Driving this wild, beautiful stretch of Chihuahuan Desert on FM 170 is the best way to understand how the border, in essence, is an abstraction.
</td></tr>
</table>

Farm-to-Market 170 is a two-lane road that roughly connects Terlingua and the nearby Big Bend National Park to Presidio, a border town roughly 60 miles to the west. Locals call this lonely ribbon of highway River Road, and as you drive, it tumbles and drops and ambles next to and above the muddy Rio Grande. Flip on the AM radio and you'll hear that most of the stations are Mexican, but don't spend too much time fiddling with the controls; your eyes are needed on the road, where the twists [and one of the steepest grades in the state] require your full attention. You'll pass the giant Big Bend Ranch State Park, where travelers can traverse a hundred miles of hike and bike trails in remote desert wilderness.

<table>
<tr><td>DAY
4</td><td>

EL PASO

An urban harbor in rugged far West Texas, witness to a back-and-forth flow of binational residents.
</td></tr>
</table>

TIME	ACTIVITY
9 AM	Wake up at modern Stanton House and grab a Savage Goods coffee, then LUCY'S CAFE for huevos rancheros.
11 AM	Trost-hop: downtown spot dozens of the architect's designs, including O.T. BASSETT TOWER, Alhambra Theatre.
1 PM	Make friends with a local, set off for sister-city CIUDAD JUÁREZ just across Bridge of the Americas; an El Recreo beer, street tacos, Kentucky Club margarita, visit to Our Lady of Guadalupe are worth long return wait [30 minutes-2 hours]; bring change, passport.
4 PM	Afternoon pan dulce pick-me-up from BOWIE BAKERY; enjoy at top of Scenic Drive overlook.
6 PM	A bar town: Head to divey MONARCH, punk Lowbrow Palace, classic Tap Bar.

EAST TEXAS

Pull back the Pine Curtain for the perfect pecan pie, a secluded wellness retreat in a '30s-era mansion and small-town charm.

TEMP
78 HIGH, 56 LOW

SUNRISE
6:51 AM

SUNSET
7:41 PM

RAINY DAYS PER MONTH
6

TRIP COST
$800 FOR 2

SEASONAL ACTIVITIES
FOOTBALL, CRAWFISH

Written off as longleaf pines and not much else, those maligned forests conceal a trove of Texas treasures. Its idyllic small towns are at once both trapped in time and thoroughly modern; its people clamor to talk about the area's potential no matter if they're an old-timer or a young transplant; and its backroads look to so much more than evergreens from cypress-studded lakes to flowered meadows. Get in on the secret before it will undoubtedly be out.

DAY
1

PALESTINE For those who dream of handing in their two weeks' notice and setting up shop somewhere bucolic, dogwood tree-dotted Palestine [pronounced "Pah-le-steen"] is dangerously enchanting. With the most National Register historic markers in the state, the neighborhoods in this railroad town abound with Victorian mansions and cute cottages; downtown with Romanesque stone buildings and a Spanish Colonial theater. Searching for the quintessential slice of Texas pecan pie? Mother-son-owned OXBOW BAKERY, once an old country store, has the crispiest crust and a praline-like filling. Time travelers, buy a ticket at the TEXAS STATE RAILROAD depot to ride in the elegant glass-top dome car 25 miles through the Piney Woods to nearby Rusk.

DAY 2 **JACKSONVILLE** Just 30 miles northeast, Jacksonville was called "the Tomato Capital of the World" in the 1950s, and residents still throw their TOMATO FEST every June, where the world record for the largest bowl of salsa was set in 2010 [and endures]. From healing stones and typewriters to antique dolls and coins, THE MUSEUM OF VANISHING TEXANA displays relics of the area's past. Improbably in this sleepy city, the HOTEL RITUAL—a pristinely preserved 1932 mansion with arched porticos, vaulted ceilings, a sauna, a swimming pool and a spa—has the attention to detail and mystique of a miniature Chateau Marmont. Owner and ayurvedic follower Whitney Graham Carter also operates a luncheonette and yoga studio downtown by the same name. Try another contender for the best pecan pie at SADLER'S. Proprietor-chef Rob Gowin's mother still makes them all by hand. Don't skip his mac and cheese.

DAY 3 **TYLER** What tomatoes are to Jacksonville, roses are to Tyler, the largest city in the pines. But the tidy, fragrant gardens and the annual Rose Queen coronation don't totally set the town's tone. New energy vibrates through Tyler too. Apothecary enthusiasts, pop into MOON RIVER NATURALS for groovy-nouveau soaps, serums and oils. Grab an Americano from the window at aluminum coffee camper Café 1948 and head to SOLA BREAD CO. for hearth-baked loaves and pastries that owner Blaine Davis learned to bake growing up in Brazil. Meet the locals later at TRUE VINE BREWING COMPANY over a Red Dirt kölsch.

BLIND LEMON JEFFERSON MEMORIAL CEMETERY
N 3rd St, Wortham

SILVER GRIZZLY ESPRESSO
100 W Tyler St, Longview silvergrizzlyespresso.com

LONESOME PINE HOME
205 Worth St, Hemphill

PEARL'S KITCHEN
207 N Madison Ave, Mount Pleasant pearlskitchentx.com

MOSS FLOWER SHOP
237 S Broadway Ave, Tyler welovemoss.com

INCLUDING

096	*Cynta de Narvaez*
098	*Randy Rodgers*
099	*Rosa Guerrero*
100	*Deborah Roberts*
102	*Noël Wells*
103	*Scott L. Nicol*
104	*Lloyd Maines*
106	*Peggy Wehmeyer*
107	*Thaddeus Cleveland*
108	*Trong Nguyen*
110	*Krishaun Adair*
111	*James Aldrete*
112	*"Tootsie" Tomanetz*
114	*Lendon Partain*
116	*Carlos Zubiate*

INTERVIEWS

Fifteen conversations with locals
of note about family history,
vocational pursuits and the
places they call home

CYNTA DE NARVAEZ

RIVER GUIDE

I BOUGHT MY place in Terlingua for $2,500. It took me 16 years to build this house.

BACK THEN, there were four houses. We were all river guides.

I'M NOT MARRIED, never have been. I'm surrounded by guides who are not married.

WHEN WE WERE fresh fruit, we picked the river over partners.

I WAS BORN in New York City, and my dad's Cuban.

HE COULDN'T FIGURE out why he killed himself to come to the United States and, you know, have a princess of a daughter who didn't want that life, right?

I DID NOT want that life.

I MOVED TO Santa Fe in 1978. I did a river trip and the guides said, "This is what you should be doing."

MY FIRST JOB as a river guide was in the Grand Canyon.

IF YOU GO to a new river and you're a guy and you make a mistake, you'll be fine. If you're a girl and you make a mistake, you're a chick.

I CAME HERE to row. I came to play in the park.

YOU CAN STILL play unsupervised here.

THE DESERT IS intense and extreme and real.

IT PUTS MILLIMETERS on your backbone.

YOU NOTICE THE quiet, and you notice the people who can sit with the silence.

AT 7:28 A.M., the sun is going to come over that hill and if this earth is going to spin at 1,040 miles per hour, don't you think we ought to be up and watch that first point of light?

RANDY RODGERS

FOOTBALL RECRUITER

IN AMERICA, it's a trickle-down sport. You emulate the big colleges. But in Texas, it starts with high school football.

WE MOVED TO Austin in 1992 when John Mackovic got the head job at Texas. I was his recruiting coordinator.

GUYS WITH THESE 900 numbers for recruiting would bombard my cellphone for scoops.

DAVE CAMPBELL started his kickoff magazine about football in 1960.

IT'S THE BIBLE in Texas. Especially for the dads.

DAVE MAILED OUT forms to all the coaches, and they'd fill out who they thought were the best prospects. If you didn't respond, he'd print, "Information not provided by high school coach."

MY SON JONNY tore his ACL as a sophomore at Westlake. His backup was Drew Brees.

I WAS A walk-on at Illinois, and my dad was a dairy farmer. Leaving the farm for an away game was impossible.

WHEN I WAS let go from UT, two of our sons were playing in college and I didn't want to miss it. That's why I started my business.

I HAD 62 colleges as clients.

THE EYEBALL TEST is a big deal.

HIT FIVE schools and two practices a day—Tuesday, Wednesday, Thursday—and write up reports every Friday.

I HEAR stories about the old days. Supposedly Eric Dickerson got a Trans Am to sign with A&M, and he drove it right to SMU the next day. Ken Dabbs, who was Darrell Royal's recruiter, lived in a Holiday Inn for 17 nights in a row trying to get Earl Campbell.

THE PAGEANTRY, the rivalries, these little towns across Texas. Nothing compares, truly.

ROSA GUERRERO

EDUCATOR, DANCER

WE LEARN FROM the past, from our grandparents and great-grandparents.

....

MY GRANDMOTHER came into Juárez in 1912 with Pancho Villa. She was the nanny.

....

MATRIARCH of matriarch. And her name was Rosa, like me. I still have her metate. The metate is a long slate you use to make your tamales.

....

I WAS BORN and raised in El Paso. In this home 60 years. I learned English because of music.

....

WE WERE PUNISHED for speaking Spanish. My mouth was washed with soap.

....

YOU KNOW, on the border we're kind of in limbo. We're American and we're Mexican—and sometimes neither.

....

MY FATHER GAVE me history, music. My mother gave me the spirit, the movement. Confidence you can do it.

IN THE '30S, during the Depression, there was no work, so my father became Mr. Mom. All those fathers took care of the children while the women worked on the border as housekeepers.

....

I WENT TO college and majored in dance. I taught modern dance, but also folk dance, folklórico. I taught English as a second language. In 1970, I started the intercultural programs.

....

MY FATHER and mother were, they were party animals. They could dance anything—polkas, schottisches, mazurkas, waltzes, bossa novas, rumbas.

....

THEY WOULD TAKE me to Juárez. Everybody came to Juárez. I knew every pasodoble. A pasodoble is a double-timed step that is fast.

....

ALL DANCE STARTS with a basic walk. Then a little run, then a skip, then hops. One, two, three, four, one, two, three, four.

DEBORAH ROBERTS

ARTIST

MY FATHER'S from Lockhart, barbecue heaven. My parents would push us in the car, all eight kids, and go down to visit my grandparents.

SAUSAGE AND CRACKERS for the kids, and the parents would eat ribs and brisket.

ALL THE WAY down the road, we had a picnic within the car.

AFTER WE ATE, we went to sleep. When we woke up, we were home, in Austin.

DRAWING WAS something that didn't belong to anybody else in my family.

ANYTIME I GOT an art tablet, it was my own special place to go away to.

I HAD GOOD teachers who pushed me. I always wanted to be an artist.

IN THE SIXTH grade, we were bused. I knew I was black, but I didn't know I was, like, black black. That's the first time that I knew being the other was something that was looked upon negatively.

I DIDN'T UNDERSTAND what it was like to be a black artist until I saw Henry O. Tanner's banjo player—in a museum pamphlet.

I FIND FACES that speak to me and could speak to others. I collage those faces.

THE COLLAGE WORK that I do is trying to explore those dark cavities that exist in people's reality.

SO MUCH OF blackness is chopped up so that it can be consumed by the other.

WHEN I DID work at the Studio Museum in Harlem, Beyoncé and Jay-Z got a preview, and they purchased work. And besides, she's a Texan.

THAT'S THE GRAVY. It's always going to be about keeping the work really good and tight.

NOËL WELLS

ACTOR

I DON'T WAIT around for anybody to give me a green light.

WHEN I THINK about filmmakers in Texas, like Richard Linklater, there's this feeling of "just go do it. No one is going to tell you no."

IT'S THE ARCHETYPE of the cowboy and the turf that he earns.

I WAS BORN in San Antonio, moved to Boerne when I was 7, then Victoria for middle and high school.

EVERYBODY SAID, "We understand you're not quite jelling here. One day you can escape to Austin."

MY MOM BOUGHT a double-wide trailer and they put it together themselves. Then we bought a house. The steps, earning your way up, that was embedded in me.

IT'S VERY TEXAN to earn your way up.

MY FOURTH-GRADE class made the school newspaper. We spent the whole year reporting, interviewing people, making comics.

IT WAS THE first time I was like, "Oh. You can just make anything."

I TEND TO dare myself to do weird things.

RIGHT BEFORE my *Saturday Night Live* audition I was in Central Park, and I walked up to these two people, and I asked if I could do the audition for them. I did, and honestly, that was scarier than doing it for the head SNL writers.

I HAD A meeting, and the audition, and it was as simple as that.

I FILMED *Mr. Roosevelt* and *Social Animals* in Austin. It's where I first picked up guitar.

WHEN I AM working on other people's films, I'm like, "What can I do?" That's how I learn.

AS TIME GOES on, my relationship with Texas shifts.

SCOTT L. NICOL

CONSERVATIONIST, ARTIST

I GREW UP outside of Dallas and Houston, and ended up in the Rio Grande Valley in 2002. I live in McAllen.

IT'S PROBABLY THE quietest place I've ever lived.

THE VALLEY IS fascinating. There's a great mixing of ecological systems and species. You're close to the coast, and as you get a little farther to the west, it dries up and is more desert-like.

THE WATER IS clean and clear. Last summer, I went out there and we canoed and spent the night next to the river. I forgot my tent. My daughter and I just slung hammocks.

HISTORICALLY, there's been a lot of movement back and forth across the border between people and families.

THE WALLS ARE really easy to climb. It takes less than a minute.

OVER TIME, I've seen the militarization of the border occur.

FLOODING and habitat fragmentation are going to be the two biggest issues, both for walls that are already up and for ones that are planned.

THERE'S A VIBRANT arts community down here, some really amazing artists, a lot better artists than me.

I DO SCULPTURES using native tree branches—ebony or Mexican olive trees. They have appendages that look kind of like sails.

OCELOTS—which are these beautiful little wild cats—can get from one patch of forest to another by following the river.

YEARS AGO AT the Santa Ana National Wildlife Refuge, I saw an ocelot. It just sat there and looked at me for about 10 minutes. I didn't move.

LLOYD MAINES

MUSICIAN, PRODUCER

SINCE I STARTED in 1973, I've produced or played on 4,000 records.

I'M NOT A heavy-handed producer.

I LEARNED TO play guitar when I was 13. Willie had a steel player named Jimmy Day. I would watch every move.

FRANK CARTER MADE my first pedal steel. He was in my father's band, the Maines Brothers.

YOU PLAY THE pedal steel with a stainless steel bar in your left hand. Two finger picks and a thumb pick on your right.

IT'S A LITTLE like watching someone play a musical sewing machine.

IF YOU'RE LUCKY, you have your brain in there some-where, once you get over the hump of not making it sound like you're killing cats.

TERRY ALLEN'S *Lubbock* [*on everything*] and *For the Last Time* by Bob Wills—those records make me want to listen over and over.

IN TEXAS, people want to dance. For some reason, people always dance counterclockwise.

ONE TIME, I got the mic. "OK, everybody stop. I want to see what happens if you all start dancing clockwise." It looked like a pinball machine.

BUDDY HOLLY wasn't embraced by Lubbock until he died.

THERE ARE NO lakes, no mountains. You kind of have to create your own entertainment.

I WAS WORKING at Caldwell Studios when I met Joe Ely in 1970. He was playing with The Flatlanders.

MY DAUGHTER NATALIE always wanted to be a singer.

....

ON VACATIONS, WE'D all listen to James Taylor cassettes, the three girls and me doing harmonies.

....

I REMEMBER WATCHING the Dixie Chicks record their first album, *Wide Open Spaces*. I had my pedal steel. She was probably 21.

....

ON STAGE, NATALIE is a fireball. She is a force. My wife and my daughters are all strong women.

....

WHAT A FORTUNATE guy I am.

PEGGY WEHMEYER

RELIGION REPORTER

WHEN I WENT off to the University of Texas, all I wanted to do was to find out what was true.

....

MY FATHER RAN off with his secretary when I was 7, and, over my lifetime, he divorced five times. It was a crazy home, an upside-down view of life.

....

I'M AN IRREGULAR verb. I'm a doubting Thomas.

....

THE HEBREW WORD for "Israel," translated, means to struggle with God.

....

IN THE '70s, the whole Jesus movement was radically different than what I learned growing up. It was rebellion.

....

I WAS THE FIRST TV reporter in America to develop a religion beat. For 20 years I was able to ask every provocative question of God I could think of.

....

CULTS AND RELIGIOUS movements. Gender and sexuality. Wherever religion meets culture is a big story. The most controversial one I did was with a group of nurses in Fort Worth who were experiencing PTSD from delivering late term abortions.

....

WE TOOK SHIFTS in Waco. I remember the FBI did weird things to antagonize them, like booming the sound of babies crying at night.

....

CULTS OFFER instant, intense community.

....

WHY AM I HERE? Why did this happen to me? Who loves me? These are the human questions that suffering forces us to face.

....

THE EVANGELICAL CHURCH is so afraid of where culture is going. Fear has led them to turn faith into a political weapon.

....

FOX NEWS, TRUMP. Families are being split over it.

....

I THINK ABOUT walking under that tower at the University of Texas, so young. It said, "Ye shall know the truth and the truth shall make you free."

THADDEUS CLEVELAND

BORDER PATROL AGENT

I'M ASSIGNED to the Sanderson Border Patrol station, which is just east of Big Bend National Park.

THE BIG BEND sector is responsible for 517 miles of border with Mexico; the Sanderson station, which I am in charge of, patrols 91 miles of it.

IT'S THE ROUGHEST terrain along the southwest border, full of limestone bluffs, mesquite and cactus, and all kinds of animals.

THE RIO GRANDE is only 20 miles away, but it takes about three hours to get there.

OFTEN, WE WORK alone. The radios are our lifeline.

ONE OF OUR main tasks is "cutting for sign"—looking for footprints left on dirt roads or trails that the smuggling organizations utilize.

WE PREDOMINANTLY come across people looking to come north to work. We haven't seen a narcotic load in three or four years.

THEY'RE WALKING 60, 70, 80, 90, a hundred miles. Heat exhaustion comes into play, so we take part in lifesaving rescues.

WHEN WE SEE these kids that come from Guatemala or Honduras by themselves, at 12, 13, 14 years old—it breaks your heart.

WE HAVE TO do the job that we swore an oath to do.

THESE SMALL TOWNS out in the Big Bend are still the best places in America to raise kids.

I STARTED MY career in Arizona, and have spent some time in D.C., but like every proud Texan, I came home.

IT TOOK ME a while to get used to the peace and quiet and hearing the freight trains rolling through. But before you know it, those just kind of blur out.

TRONG NGUYEN

RESTAURATEUR

WE MAKE VIET-CAJUN at Crawfish & Noodles. It's French colony food—the spice from Vietnam with the Louisiana Cajun sauce. Then there's the garlic butter. That's French.

YOU WANT TO taste the freshness of the crawfish inside with the seasoning coating the outside.

ON THE WEEKEND, we can go through 700 to 1,000 pounds of crawfish.

I CAME TO the States in 1987 as a refugee.

WHEN I WAS a kid, I would always be with my grandmother.

I TASTED what she cooked before she brought it to the table for the family.

BEFORE WE OPENED the business in 2008, I would cook for my family. That taste from her is in me. The way she would put sugar or black pepper on something.

I WENT TO school for computers but ended up going to work at the casino. Going from the computer to the casino is kind of weird, but everything is related.

I WAS PART of a team that opened a casino in Louisiana. That's how I learned about Cajun food: boudin, jambalaya, alligator on a stick.

I JOINED TILMAN Fertitta and we opened the Golden Nugget in Las Vegas.

WHEN WE OPENED the restaurant, I was still working for the casino. But you can't have two feet on both sides. So that's how I became a full-time chef.

WE HAVE A lot of fan love. It is something I never expected.

FIFTEEN YEARS AGO, this street was nothing. Now it has so many restaurants and so many different kinds of food.

THAT'S THE LOVE in Houston.

KRISHAUN ADAIR

BARREL RACER

RODEO WAS INTRODUCED to me through the generations. That passion was handed down.

I SPECIALIZE IN barrel racing and steer decorating.

THREE 55-gallon drums are set in the middle of the arena in a cloverleaf pattern.

IT'S OVER IN less than 15 seconds.

THERE ISN'T barrel racer alive that doesn't have scars on her legs.

NINE TIMES OUT of 10, if she's a barrel racer, she's gonna have on a long dress.

YOU KNOCK OVER a barrel and people think "Oh a 5-second penalty." That's a 55-gallon metal barrel.

EVEN IN FRONT of 20,000 people, you want it to feel like it's just you and your horse.

YOU HAVE TO know how to win and know how to lose.

NO MATTER HOW trained a horse is, they can still be unpredictable.

SOME OF MY mother's best advice was, "They are only going to pay you one time for that run." Go back like it never happened and then do it again.

THAT'S WHAT MAKES you a champion and not just a winner.

YOU CAN WIN thousands of dollars, saddles, gold buckles, but can only wear one at a time.

THE MEMORIES ARE made on the road. You spend more time in the truck than on a horse.

I WORK FOR the state and am in the field a lot. They don't know what I do on the weekend.

I WILL TEACH my daughter, who's 4, that if rodeo is where her heart lies, she'll be successful at it.

NONE OF YOUR successes come from you alone.

JAMES ALDRETE

POLITICAL CONSULTANT

DAD WAS PART of desegregating public schools, through West Texas. He was the first Mexican American city councilman in Del Rio, then county attorney.

HE MOVED US to D.C. to work for the DNC, on what was supposed to be the re-election for President Johnson.

WE'D PACK FIVE kids in a car and drive 2,000 miles to borderland. Mom had to see her sisters.

I GOT AN internship with the Democratic Senatorial Campaign Committee—going through fiche files, doing opposition research. It was awesome.

GERRYMANDERING has always happened.

IT'S CALLED CRACKING and packing. They pack Hispanics and African-Americans into as few seats as possible. Then they crack and dilute their voice. What you get is very few contested general elections.

WHEN YOU overemphasize how many generations you've been here, you're basically saying, "I'm not that immigrant."

YARD SIGNS DON'T vote. It is very much a psychological game about how you keep your own supporters motivated. In South Texas you put your photo on it. San Antonio's big on the neon colors shining at night.

DESPITE broad pride in Texas, we really could be five different states.

IT'S BEEN CLOSE to 30 years since we've been a competitive state. Now it's starting to change. Even at the congressional level we're going to be picking up seats.

IT'S ALWAYS FUN to go back and watch Ann Richards versus Clayton Williams. His commercials were all about riding horses.

SHE HAD THE work ethic. She could reach back into old Texas, reach forward into new Texas. Her voice was strong.

"TOOTSIE" TOMANETZ

PITMASTER, GROUNDSKEEPER

THIS IS MY 23rd year working at the school. The barbecue is Saturday.

I DO NOT consider myself 84.

CLAY COWGILL IS with the pit all night adding wood—dried post oak. I get there at 2 a.m.

BACK IN 1966, my husband, White, was working at City Meat Market in Giddings. The owner, Hershel Doyle, asked, "Do you think Tootsie would help Orange in the pit?"

I KNEW HOW to read a scale and I could count change. I didn't know the meats. I was there 10 years.

MR. DOYLE BOUGHT a meat market in Lexington. It was my baby to take care of.

I REALLY WENT into it not thinking that I was different than anyone else. Sweat running down my face. Customers would come in, "Oh you poor dear." I would say, "I hadn't really realized. I've been busy."

AT THE OLD market in Lexington, Kerry Bexley would come in for lunch. I saw him grow up.

WE SOLD THE market in 1996 when White had his stroke. The people who bought it asked me if I would continue cooking. A few days later, Kerry Bexley asked, "How about we open a barbecue place?"

I SAID, "I've committed to them. But should the time come that I'm not happy, you will be the first person I talk to."

MARCH 1, 2003, was Snow's opening date.

LATELY, I'VE NOTICED I'm not as strong in my lifting. Fifty pounds is easy. Used to be nothing for me to put a 150-pound quarter of beef on the block.

I'M VERY SINCERE when I say I've been doing this for 50-plus years but I'm still learning.

I KNOW I won't live forever. I hope I can work until I just can't.

LENDON PARTAIN

OIL FIELD TECHNICIAN

THE PERMIAN BASIN is a really beautiful place. But you do have to try harder. It doesn't look like Ireland.

A WELL DIAGNOSTIC technician works with wells after they've been drilled. I'm doing all of the in-depth maintenance. I'm shooting fluid levels.

FOR A MANUAL labor job to be about fluid mechanics and thermodynamics, that's awesome. It's a thinking man's thing. I love the ideas.

WE'RE 100 MILES south of Lubbock, 30 miles north of Odessa. Up until the '40s, Andrews was ranching.

MY GRANDFATHER started pumping in the '60s. I started going around with him at 5 years old, same thing with my dad—because, child care, really. Going around with them, and learning from them, and hearing the history.

AS SOON AS I was able to sneak off and drive to the wells at 15 or 16, I was out there: staging tanks, doing pipe work, roustabout-y stuff, changing out valves.

EVERY ONE OF my friends in Odessa and Andrews, they're all working like that.

I'VE HAD WELLS that my grandpa took care of and now I do.

IT'S WHAT YOU would ecologically call an ecotone of desert grassland or savanna.

A WELL PAD takes up less than an acre. Within a square mile, there's only going to be maybe 40 wells. All around, there's places for wildlife.

I GOT MY degree in ecology and evolutionary biology, my master's in molecular biology.

MY THESIS WAS on *Hemileuca slosseri*, a moth that's only found in, like, nine counties.

And they're almost all in the oil field.

HOW DID THEY ever get naturally selected? To handle an extreme of a hundred-degree difference? And they have to do that in three different phases of their life cycle.

A MESQUITE TREE, it's almost like in the rainforest. There's this whole biome there. I've seen up to 30 species on a mesquite tree—that's fricking awesome. There's more than meets the eye.

ANYBODY—a production lease operator, or pumper, or whatever—they all will tell you, "Man, sometimes when I'm done with work, I just go walking out there."

NOT VERY MANY places you can go make $100,000. Any guy off the street could, if they're smart and can pick it up.

I'M NOT GETTING paid anything extra for my degree, you know what I mean?

THE FIRST BITS of a boom, everybody kind of jumps the gun and does all sorts of crazy stuff.

PEOPLE LIKE US, we understand what's going to happen. We're always here. Whereas you've got guys that go, "Woohoo, party, I made $10,000 in two weeks."

YOU'VE GOT TO remember there's still people working at Pizza Hut. It's not like there's not enough housing. It's just that nobody can afford it.

WHEN A WELL'S being drilled, dude, you get adrenaline. Everything I work on out there is a million dollars. And it is exciting—knowing that you're pretty good at it.

THERE'S a camaraderie. Just like in a war, in a way, but we know we're winning the war. It's a weird thing.

CARLOS ZUBIATE

CONCIERGE

I WAS BORN in El Paso. My mom moved to Juárez when I was months old. She's from Durango originally.

SUMMERS, we stayed up till 1 a.m. playing soccer in the streets.

ONCE I FINISHED elementary school, I was sent to live with one of my aunts in El Paso.

A LOT OF children are of two worlds. Always going over the border.

IF YOU COME to this particular spot between 6 and 7 a.m., you'll see hundreds of students crossing the bridge.

WHEN WE DIDN'T have any change to pay for the bridge toll, we'd load, like, 15, 20 of us onto the back of the truck.

WE'RE ABOUT TO go into El Paso and it's going to take at least an hour to get there. It can be hard.

MY MOM'S PART of the maquiladora industry, factories.

MY FAVORITE DISH, nopales—basically cactus in red chile sauce with pork and rice, with flour tortillas.

AT 6 YEARS old, I went over to buy some gorditas and was hit by a hearse. I could not get out of bed for a good eight months, and my mother had to teach me how to read and write.

I JOINED THE Navy straight out of high school. It was the first time I ever boarded a plane.

I WENT TO that Walmart often. When we saw the news, I was in the hotel. The kitchen, everybody was texting all their family members. I was thinking the whole time, it has to be somebody not from here.

WHY WOULD ANYONE come here and do something like that?

INCLUDING

120   **LANDSCAPE OF SOUND**
By Kimberly King Parsons

128   **A VIEW FROM THE WATER**
By Stephen Harrigan

134   **LAS SILUETAS**
By Octavio Solis

143   **WE HATE TO SEE THE SUN GO**
By Lady Bird Johnson

STORIES

Essays and recollections
from noted Texan voices

LANDSCAPE OF SOUND

Written by **KIMBERLY KING PARSONS**

THEY SAY MOST people can't actually pinpoint their very first memory, but I swear I came to consciousness in the frigid back seat of my mother's gold Buick, on a highway between Lubbock and Turkey. It is summertime and I'm 3 years old, bouncing around to "Sway," my favorite Rolling Stones song. It's my dad's favorite too, which is why he puts it on every road trip mixtape. I'm unbuckled, loose on the leatherette bench seat—child passenger safety laws are still a couple years away—and I'm holding a cherry slush from Allsup's between my thighs. My dad is driving, my mom asleep next to him. I'm pressing on my closed eyelids to the beat of the music—this strange thing I still sometimes do—triggering hot pink flashes and fluorescent bursts, my own internal pyrotechnics show. Mick Jagger is asking, "Did you ever wake up to find / A day that broke up your mind / Destroyed your notion of circular time?" Somewhere in this moment, or, OK, fine, in an amalgam of moments like this one, I realize I'm here—I've slipped into my body and the world of myself, officially and irrevocably me.

My parents moved to Lubbock just before I was born, but our big extended family—grandparents, more than 30 aunts and uncles, what feels like a hundred cousins—still lives in my dad's hometown of Turkey [and neighboring Quitaque, pronounced "Kitty-quay," my mom's equally tiny birthplace]. Our blood relatives make up a not-insignificant chunk of the total population of this part of the state— the buckle of the Bible Belt—and we are always going back to visit them.

My dad says you need two things to stay alive when you drive through the Panhandle: air conditioning and loud music. The AC is obvious enough—our summer temperatures swelter into triple digits—but my dad believes music keeps all that vast, flat terrain from messing with your mind. Our family joke is that 207-N is the road from nowhere to nowhere, but there's something magical about this featureless landscape too. There are these steaming, harmless mirages that disappear when you look at them, but you also hear about full-on hallucinations that cause cars to swerve and brake: phantom motorcycles and false pedestrians, impossible animals loping into the road. Eighteen-wheelers jackknife for no real reason, spew out their glittery mess.

Besides keeping us safe, my dad's mixtapes serve as the soundtrack to the Panhandle: the Stones, the Beatles, the Kinks, a rotating lineup of his lifelong favorites. This part of Texas is a sea of tan nothing, the backdrop a case study in dusty isolation. The wide spaces beg for a song; the dull, unspooling scrub turns eerie and beautifully lunar if set to the right music. When I'm a little older, my dad will teach me about the British Invasion—the bands I'll already know, but the details will be new. He'll fully indoctrinate me on these road trips, quiz me about dead drummers, studio guitarists, songwriting credits. In the Buick, we'll mostly listen to bands from abroad, but outside the car, the Panhandle already has its own music, a thrum that has been building, emanating from the most unlikely place: home.

It's reasonable to be suspicious when a tiny town claims a legend, but Turkey really has one. Known as the King of Western Swing, Bob Wills is born in 1905 to a family of champion fiddle players. The son of sharecroppers, he is a prodigious and motivated kid who starts playing for money at ranch dances when he is just 10 years old. His long career is influenced by country, blues and jazz, and he is among the first musicians to incorporate drums into country arrangements. In 1968, he is named into the Country Music Hall of Fame. He is [posthumously] inducted into the Rock & Roll Hall of Fame in 1999.

Turkey may not have a stoplight, but there's a wrought-iron gate that proudly declares it the "Home of Bob Wills." The town's biggest and only attempt at tourism is Bob Wills Day, which takes place every April at the Bob Wills Museum. It's true that hundreds of people come to pay their respects and dance to live Western swing, but the town is dead quiet the other 364 days a year. The museum is directly across the street from my grandmother's house, in the building that used to be the school. In 1972, the year after my mom and dad graduated, they

closed the school down because there were no longer enough young people in Turkey to justify its existence. Now Wills memorabilia is displayed in a renovated storefront, but the upper floors of the building are a perfect time capsule of my parents' senior year: There are still desks with pencils in them, stacks of textbooks on shelves. One summer when I am listless and bored and not quite a teenager, my cousin S and I will crawl through a broken basement window and engage in some trespassing and minor vandalism. We'll bring in a bucket of horny toads and set them loose in the old gym; we'll draw elaborate genitalia on the crumbling chalkboards. We won't be at all interested in the remodeled museum wing. At this point, I won't yet understand who Bob Wills is, that he's sold a million records, that he's regarded as a national treasure.

> **HE HOOTS AND YELLS AND STAMPS HIS FEET. INSTEAD OF A MAN WORKING, YOU GET TO SEE HIM AS THE CHILD HE MUST HAVE BEEN ONCE.**

My dad says he knew Wills was famous, but he had no idea how famous until much later. Growing up, my dad is too young to be a hippie, but he is deeply influenced by the pacifism and protest of the counterculture movement, and the music that accompanies those beliefs is rock and roll, not country. He considered Wills and his famous band, the Texas Playboys, to be something the older people in town liked dancing to. Not only is Western swing more his parents' musical taste, but my mom's dad [his future father-in-law] had played fiddle with Wills for several years [not as an official part of the Texas Playboys, but in the rotating band that swells or contracts depending on the size of the dance hall]. My mom's mom is a self-proclaimed Bob Wills groupie who lives for ranch dances; she jokes that she settled for my grandpa [a sweet widower who was 23 years her senior when they met] because Wills himself wasn't interested in her. My grandpa will be buried with the fiddle he played back then, he so revered his time with the band. All of these stories seem to justify the reason my dad doesn't consider Bob Wills all that relevant. Country music came to represent the twang of a place my dad hoped to escape.

When I am in a weird noise band in college, I'll try to get into

Western swing, if only to annoy my dad, but the music won't hit my heart quite right either—too old-fashioned maybe, the lyrics too sentimental or the arrangements too stiff. My favorite moments come from the live performances. Wills is known for his wisecracking, but the humor often feels rehearsed. He's a strict bandleader, and you get the feeling he's got his eye on everyone, reins tight, that every wry comment or wink is planned out to the second. But then there are moments, usually when somebody else in his band is doing a solo, when he seems to get caught up in the music. His posture changes; he hoots and yells and stamps his feet. Instead of a man working, you get to see him as the child he must have been once, open and listening, delighted.

My dad always identifies more with the musical legend from my hometown: Buddy Holly, beloved Lubbock singer, songwriter, instrumentalist, bandleader and producer. Holly was a young genius made all the more unforgettable because of his tragic death at the age of 22, when my dad was just 6 years old. He directly influenced the bands my dad loves the most: the Beatles, Dylan and, of course, the Rolling Stones.

Unlike my dad's experience with Bob Wills, when I am growing up in Lubbock, it will be impossible for me to escape how prescient and far-reaching the music of Buddy Holly is. It seems as though every relevant band cites Holly as inspiration—even the Britpop and emo groups I come to love as a semi-Goth preteen. I won't see the genius of Holly's songs at first because they are so deceptively simple, and because so many other acts have pillaged his sound, lifted his arrangements and chord progressions whole cloth over the years. His biggest hits sound like television commercials to me, some jingle that is trying to get me to buy a car or eat a box of cereal. To me, Buddy Holly is the deadest of dead guys, memorialized by that silly statue across from the strip mall, his big glasses ghostly and creepy. Some kids call for Bloody Mary in their dark bathroom mirrors, but at slumber parties in Lubbock, we screamed for Peggy Sue. It will take me decades to understand that a good pop song is nothing short of magic—that sticking a melody in somebody's ear is a miracle.

When my dad is growing up in Turkey, he thinks of Lubbock as the big city: a chic, bustling metropolis in the middle of a cotton field. This is certainly an overstatement, but the differences between my childhood and his are staggering. I'll be raised in a suburban neighborhood near the university. I'll go to private school and summer camp; I'll take guitar lessons, which I'll hate, and piano lessons, which I'll love. But I'm ungrateful; to me, Lubbock is howling wind, sandstorms and haunting boredom, a place I dream of leaving.

Soon, a different Texas sound will light up my brain. In high school, somebody's big sister plays a record at a party, and my world cracks open. I can't tell if the singer is in ecstasy or agony, if it's a man or a woman, if it's a machine; I can't tell if there is one person or three or 10 in the band, if "band" is even the right word. The music is set to an unstoppable drumbeat, but I can't tell what other instruments are being played, if one of them is maybe a chain saw or a drill or if there's just something wrong with the speakers at this party. I will later learn I'm listening to the band's most melodic and accessible record, and that they are best known for live shows so intense and disorienting they make the audience puke.

"What *is* this?" I ask the older girl.

"The Surfers," she'll say, and later I'll wonder if she was afraid to say the full name out loud.

The Butthole Surfers are from down in San Antonio, and like all my favorite bands, I come in too late, at the tail end of their long career, the exact opposite of the pretentious record store stereotype. I buy the latest release; the cover shows a pencil being shoved into an ear.

"This isn't music," my dad will say, and that's how I'll know I'm onto something good.

I've grown up with "Lucy in the Sky With Diamonds," but the Butthole Surfers will help me find a specifically psychedelic Texas—not new maybe, but new to me—a kind of primer not only for the music I love most, but for the wonderfully weird, lysergic perspective that will color everything I come to believe about art-making. For a while at least, I won't feel so restless, so eager to leave.

In college, after somebody teaches me about psilocybin mushrooms in cow paddies, I will feel a precise counterpoint to my earliest memory. I'm moving through those familiar flat plains, this time on foot. I'm with a group of friends instead of my parents, and our chosen soundtrack is playing. Suddenly, instead of coming into myself, I will feel the self gracefully obliterated, poured out. At the same time, I will feel tied to the land, tangled up in Texas in the best way. I will finally be able to see my home state for the big, beautiful canvas it is—a landscape that's huge enough to hold every kind of sound.

KIMBERLY KING PARSONS is the author of the story collection *Black Light*, longlisted for both the 2019 National Book Award and the 2019 Story Prize. Her work has been published by *The Paris Review*, *Black Warrior Review* and *Electric Lit*.

A VIEW FROM THE WATER

Written by **STEPHEN HARRIGAN** | **A COASTAL MORNING** in winter. The gray light filtering down from behind a mackerel sky onto the steely surface of the bay. Brown pelicans and cormorants crowded together on a patch of oyster reef; an osprey perched on top of a channel marker as it tears apart a fish; dolphin fins appearing in the still waters of the intracoastal canal like shears slicing through silk.

I wonder how many casual readers, encountering the paragraph I've just written about an unspecified seacoast, would ever think to apply it to Texas. Shorelines and shorebirds, dolphins and oyster reefs have never been part of the go-to iconography of the Lone Star State. For advertisers and art directors, the default descriptors are still cowboy hats, bucking broncos, oil wells and parched landscapes with windmills and cow skulls.

But this is Texas too, these flat coastal marshes where an excursion boat named *Skimmer* is quietly nosing up to a riprap shoreline so that we tourists can get a view of one of the rarest and most endangered birds in the world. The only wild migrating flock of whooping cranes breeds during the summer in the wetlands of northern Canada before flying 2,500 miles south to winter here in the Aransas National Wildlife Refuge. Five feet high, they are North America's tallest birds, but they're mostly feathers—they weigh only about 16 pounds. Their 7-foot wingspan terminates in distinctive black primary feathers that make them look, in flight, as if they're wearing gloves.

There are other snowy white birds in the marsh—egrets, ibis and the white pelicans that spiral down from the sky or float on the water almost everywhere you glance. And there are great blue herons and roseate spoonbills and, scrutinizing everything from its perch in a tree rising above the marsh grass, a solitary great horned owl.

This part of the Gulf Coast features an unmissable abundance of natural history, but it's arguably the most crucial locale for Texas' human history as well. It was along this expansive seashore, in 1528, that the first Europeans arrived in the land that would eventually become known as Texas. It was in the bayous and marshlands at the upper end of Galveston Bay that Texas seized its independence from Mexico at the Battle of San Jacinto. Nine years later, after the Republic of Texas joined the Union, the coastal settlement of Corpus Christi served as the staging ground for the American incursion into Mexico, a war that increased the size of the United States by a third and created a new crisis over the expansion of slavery that resulted in the Civil War. And in 1901, only about 40 miles inland, the country's first gusher came in at Spindletop, ushering in the age of oil and American industrial might.

This is not to diminish the economic or cultural importance of the rest of the state's 261,000 square miles. The wars of previous centuries between Spaniards and Native Americans, between Mexicans and Native Americans, between Anglos and Mexicans, between Anglos and Native Americans, between each of the above against all of the others, sprawled all over Texas and distilled its past into its present. The trail drives that passed through the western and northern parts of the state beginning in the 1870s were important factors in creating a mythic cowboy culture and an expanding economy, as was the invention of the integrated circuit in Dallas less than a century later. And though oil was first discovered at Spindletop, it is the Permian Basin, in West Texas, that has turned out, thanks to hydraulic fracturing, to be the most productive field in the world.

There's a reason that West Texas, in particular, has for so long pulled focus from the rest of the state and has been, for most people who know Texas only from movies and rumors, its defining ground. It's the Texas of the once-open range and—despite the wind farms on every bluff and mesa—still-open sky. It's a place that has been brewed up out of a hunger for romantic desolation, the Texas of *The Last Picture Show* and *Lonesome Dove*, of Cormac McCarthy novels and mournful country ballads.

The city of Abilene, where I was partly raised, was near the epicenter of that trope-rich Texas territory. When my family left Oklahoma and moved to Abilene in 1953, there were still people in the city who were alive during, and maybe even had childhood memories of, the great buffalo slaughter, or the trail drives, or the final years of Comanche resistance. Even as a 6- or 7-year-old kid, I had a sense that history was barely history yet—it was still part of the living past. The flat plains and low hills that spread out from the city did not constitute what any reasonable person would consider scenery. But the harshness and emptiness of the landscape, the fact that there was nothing to see, sharpened your curiosity both about what might be beyond the horizon and what might be lying at your feet. All the buildings were new, and there were no ancient temples or cathedrals to suggest that deep time had ever existed here, but there was a good chance, if you looked carefully and dug along creek banks where there had once been Indian encampments, of finding arrowheads and spearpoints.

LIVING IN SOUTH TEXAS BROUGHT ME INTO SUDDEN CONTACT WITH THE STATE'S MOST FATEFUL CHARACTERISTIC: IT'S 1.254-MILE BORDER WITH MEXICO.

It was hard not to be formed to some degree by living in that part of Texas, by sensing that you were part of the continuing history of the Old West. But when we moved to the coast, to Corpus Christi, there was a different juju, and for me it was even stronger. The salt air, the murky inland waters, the riotous vegetation, the wild surf, the unrelenting humidity that made you feel as though you were living in a terrarium—all of this infiltrated my bloodstream and enlarged my perceptions while conceivably altering my body chemistry.

How was it possible that this was still Texas? Finding myself set down into two such radically different environments gave me an understanding, for the first time, of how large and various Texas must be. And I still had only the vaguest sense of the state's true geographic reach. I had not yet seen the dense forests of East Texas, or the haunted monotony of the Chihuahuan Desert that stretched far beyond Abilene to the southwest.

And living in South Texas brought me into sudden contact with the state's most fateful and most ineradicable characteristic: its 1,254-mile border with Mexico. It was clear that I was not in Abilene anymore, and maybe not exactly in the United States. The territory

in South Texas between the Nueces River and the Rio Grande had been for centuries the contested ground between Texas and Mexico, and though the issue of which country owned what had supposedly been settled by the 1848 Treaty of Guadalupe Hidalgo that ended the Mexican-American War, the farther south you went in Texas the less you were convinced that Mexico had not come out ahead. The strange new food [what was a taco, exactly?], the conjunto and orquesta music that came out of the car radio, the Spanish surnames of half the kids in my elementary and high school classes: All of this contributed to a bracing cultural vibe that would have seemed utterly foreign on the West Texas Plains but that in this place felt organically dominant.

You saw it most vividly in San Antonio, the Texas city that had been the capital of Spanish Texas since the 18th century and, in its soul, had never had any intention of renouncing that identity. There was the Alamo, of course, right there in the heart of the city, the undisputed headspring of Texas history. But there was also Market Square, with its Mexican restaurants and mariachis and shops selling onyx chess sets and bullwhips and marionettes and armadillo purses—souvenirs that were as obviously cheesy as they were convincingly exotic. And the architecture not just of the Alamo but of San Antonio's four other Spanish colonial missions grounded everything in antiquity and made history visible in a way it could never have been in West Texas, where the ancient cultures were mostly nomadic and left behind no edifices, only traces in the ground.

But to the migrants from other states and other countries who arrive at its borders at the rate of about 500 a day, Texas is still mostly about the future—just as it was for Davy Crockett when he came here from Tennessee in 1835 after his political and economic fortunes collapsed, or for George H.W. Bush, when he forsook the comforts of Connecticut to try his luck in the oil business in Odessa in 1948. It has always been a place of churning opportunity, a good part of the reason it is now the second-most-populous state in the country and why, in decades to come, will likely overtake California, which is the first. It's why Houston, a place that most Americans have only the foggiest impression of, is the fourth-largest city in the United States and its most ethnically diverse, with a population that speaks 145 languages. And it's why the sacred Alamo is thought to be in constant peril of being overtaken as Texas' number-one tourist site by the Magnolia Market at the Silos, the decidedly non-sacred complex in Waco that is the retail offshoot of Chip and Joanna Gaines' TV show, *Fixer Upper*.

The interesting thing about Texas, though, is that the future never quite pulls away from the past, just as the ethnic and geographical forces that ought to have long ago broken the state into fragments have somehow done the opposite and bound it into a common identity. That's why, as the whooping crane boat pulls away from the marshlands of the Aransas National Wildlife Refuge and begins the return journey across the open bay, it's no surprise to spot, on the distant shoreline, a Lone Star flag waving in the offshore breeze.

STEPHEN HARRIGAN is a writer-at-large for *Texas Monthly* and the author of 11 books of fiction and nonfiction, of which the most recent is *Big Wonderful Thing: A History of Texas*.

LAS SILUETAS

Written by **OCTAVIO SOLIS**

ASPIRADORA, 1979

The days are long and hot. Longer and hotter than anyone can remember. El Paso is in the mouth of the summer. Every day yields a temperature over 100 degrees. And what am I doing? Selling vacuum cleaners door to door. After studying abroad for a year, I am back home trying to raise funds for my last year in college, but damned if I'm gonna head back to my old job at Chico's Tacos. No, man, I'm entitled to a better job this year.

I'm surprised, though, when I drive into this industrial park and walk into a simple office setup with about 20 other hirees. It's a company selling vacuum cleaners, the expensive brand vacs that run on water filters. For a week, we're taught everything about these vacuums: how they're made, how they work, how they fit in the box. We're drilled on how to sell them. We learn the sales spiel, so tight and cleverly constructed it almost guarantees a sale. Days begin in song. "We'll be selling 10 more vacuums when we go."

Some of the hires, mainly the women, work the phone banks, calling lists of people to tell them they've won a new prize. When will they be home to receive it? That's our way in. Once an address and a time is confirmed, the sales reps are dispatched. So here I am, driving my car all over El Paso in a coat and tie through this impossible heat. Sweat stains under my tie, on my back and armpits. Hot winds swirling dust into my face, as I carry a large heavy box containing a $,1000 vacuum cleaner from house to house.

This one afternoon, I'm looking for an address in a lower-rent neighborhood than we're usually referred to. I find the house, an old 1930s bungalow with a rickety gate held open by a potted cactus. I balance my box against my hip and hoist it toward the front door, sweat dripping from my brow. I knock on the screen door and this tiny woman, maybe 70 with clouded eyes, greets me. I tell her I'm here to deliver her prize and she looks down at my box and opens the door. Entre, por favor, she says.

Her living room is dark and sparsely furnished. Everything old but clean. A single framed photo of some grandson in a cap and gown presides over the room. A smell of something good and Mexican cooking in the kitchen. The woman tells me her name is Señora. Mariana Ponce and asks if her prize is in the box. I tell her yes and produce from inside the flap a thin bicentennial coloring book depicting chief moments in our great history. She looks at George Washington on the cover and asks, ¿Quien es esa vieja?

That's not an old lady, ma'am. That's the father of our country, George Washington.

She scowls uncertainly as she tosses the coloring book on the table. I take that as my segue.

Señora Ponce, you're very fortunate to be one of the few selected by my company for a unique demonstration of this miracle in housekeeping. May I?

Before she knows it, I thrust my vacuum cleaner demo out of the box in three pieces and assemble it before her eyes.

Ah, una aspiradora.

Para usted, señora. Launching into my practiced pitch, I tell her about the Black & Decker engine and the power of the suction and all the wonderful accoutrements. While I'm performing, and it is a performance, I monitor her reactions. Her dark pliant face, which offsets her severe expression, is immobile. The unfussiness of her wire-gray hair and her clothing matches the house. I ask her to please fill up the plastic basin with faucet water. She readily complies and while in the kitchen, I scout for a patch of carpet to run my vac through. But there's no carpet, no rug, only plain tile flooring that in some places has peeled away and exposed the concrete foundation underneath.

She returns with the basin in one hand and a plate in the other. Beans and a burrito of the guisado I smelled earlier. She urges me to continue my presentation. She sits by me; we eat and talk about the commonplace matters that press us, the heat, the cat that won't come out from under her bed, the last time her daughters dropped by. She asks me if this is what I want to do with my life. I tell her that I'm studying the craft of acting, but my real aspiration is to be a writer. I don't think I know it until I say it in that moment. Mrs. Ponce says she went to El Paso High back in the day, and that once, she thought of being a writer, too, but after she got married, that notion just flew out the window. Instead, she worked for her husband as a bookkeeper in his automotive garage. He's in Evergreen now, she says.

Now it's time to get back to my pitch. I attach the basin to the vac and demonstrate the superior strength of the suction right on the bumpy tile. The basin immediately turns muddy, which provokes a surprised look from her. I just swept that floor too, she says. After I complete my demonstration, I grudgingly run through the payment plans, which can run from 10 months to five years. It's only a formality. There's no way she can afford it. But as I finish going over the payments and turn to put the vac back in its box, I hear her sigh.

Entonces, tengo que comprarla.

Are you serious, señora? You want to buy this?

She tells me that I've plainly shown how much she needs this for her home.

But can you afford it? I say. She shrugs and replies that I've gone to all this trouble for her. She looks at me with cloudy black eyes and asks if it would help me to make this sale.

Of course, it would. But you need a credit card for the down payment.

She goes to another room to fetch her purse and returns with her Sears card. I nod and ask her to use the phone, where I finalize the deal with my supervisor. She picks up the plates and glasses with the solemn care of an old gardener. I know her credit will fail and she'll never receive the aspiradora. I think she knows that too. She asks where I am headed next. I shrug, looking down at the ugly cardboard box I've lugged around in the sun.

This is my last appointment for the day, I tell her.

HAMBURGER INN, 1969

We sit in front of the old boxy black-and-white RCA, watching the comedy shows. My sister, my little brothers and me. It's *The Flying Nun*, followed by *Bewitched* and then *That Girl*. My mom is in the kitchen trying to scare up some dinner for us. We hear her behind us banging pots and pans. My fingernails go in my mouth, which means I'm hungry.

Mom says she's tired. She's been working all day at the neighborhood soda fountain. When the commercials come on, Mom says, "Why don't we go see your dad at work?"

She calls ahead to tell him we're on our way and we pile in the Ford Galaxie. It's a shimmering Thursday night on Alameda Avenue. Cars are full with families and kids, and they're playing music so loudly we can't hear our own radio. In the distance, I see a blurry Spanish-language movie playing on the screen of the Ascarate Drive-in.

We head past the cemetery to the older stretch of Alameda, where the crumbling auto shops and grocery stores are shuttered for the night and the barred windows of the little adobe houses lining the street glow with warm lamplight. We turn left onto a side road, then down a dark alley. It opens to a gravel parking lot at the back entrance of the Hamburger Inn. Just a screen door and floodlights, but we know there's more than that. My mom refuses to set foot inside. She sends me in to ask for my dad. As the oldest, it's a right I've earned. The pride of it tingles my scalp.

I TELL HER THAT I'M STUDYING THE CRAFT OF ACTING, BUT MY REAL ASPIRATION IS TO BE A WRITER. I DON'T THINK I KNOW IT UNTIL I SAY IT IN THAT MOMENT.

I open the screen door and immediately smell hot grease and burnt onions. There is so much bustle and noise. Cooks slapping patties on the grill, the scrawny kid washing tall stacks of dishes, waitresses jostling past the customers at the counter, the jarring brrring of the cash register. People chatter away at their tables while they eat, and the jukebox is playing a Mexican ranchera by a silky-voiced tenor. I think it's my dad by the steaming pot of menudo and I call for him, but the man in the stained white shirt and paper hat is only Poncho. His paunchy face beams when he turns to see me. He makes some joke about my cowlick, causing a couple of stern-looking old men to chuckle. With his large hand, he leads me back outside and says that my dad is getting the order ready. He waves grandiosely at my mom who can't help but burst out laughing. Then Poncho goes back inside. He'll die of liver cancer about twenty years later, a pained old drunk still making us laugh.

I feel my stomach grumbling as I take my seat in the back. We sit in silence, united in our hunger. At last, the screen door opens, and my dad steps out. He is under the floodlights, in his white apron and pleated gray pants, with his steady walk and his head held high. He holds the white paper bags of burgers and fries and ice-cubed Coca-Colas. He'll never surpass this moment.

He passes the bags around, and we dig in while he and Mom trade stories of the day. We're too busy to care about their conversation, but there is one story I catch.

It was quiet earlier, he tells my mom. Not many people. This old borracho with a bag of pan dulce comes in wanting something. Couldn't understand him, he was so drunk. He got loud when Licha from the morning shift asked him to leave. Banging on the counter. I went to him and told him, Que se vaya ya. He tried to swing at me, but I moved and grabbed him from the collar. I pulled him outside and threw him on the sidewalk and told him to go home. When I went back inside, I looked through the window, and there he was on his knees, trying to pick up the pan dulce on the sidewalk. Seeing him like that, on his knees like that, I couldn't take it. So I went and picked up his bread for him and put it in the bag. And then I walked him to the bakery and bought him some more. How's your hamburguesa?

Poncho yells through the screen door that the rush has started. He better get his nalgas back to work. My father gives us each a tousle of the head. He walks toward the door and he turns back. The floodlights wash over him in his white apron and shirt, and the figure passes into a time that has no time at all.

FIONA, 2008

Practically across from UTEP, he says.

The camera guy I've hired is telling me where to go and get a close-up look of the Rio Grande. He's been around El Paso all his life and knows all the nooks that yield up the wonders and absurdities of this border town. We meet up and caravan west to where Highway 85 and Interstate 10 converge near downtown. We pull off near the UTEP campus, just as he said. We're on gravel, parked under the tiny open-air pavilions that the Border Patrol has set up for its agents, who sit in their sweltering SUVs all day. He prepares his video camera, and I look at the stark barren mountains in front of me, with the surf of freeway traffic roaring behind.

The camera guy leads me through a thicket of weeds and dried broken limbs to the water's edge. The shallow brown current moves swiftly past. There's all kinds of ducks and cormorants sunning on the small sandy shoal in a break in the river. Check it out, he says, pointing to the spillway where the rio is dammed and some of its water diverted. There's a couple of kids on the Mexican side, their hands idly picking at the chain-link fence as though it's a guitar. We better shoot this now, he says. I think they want to cross.

I take off my shoes and socks, roll up my pants and slip into the water, feeling its cool ribbons slipping through my toes. All for some footage of me walking in the river for a project in San Francisco. The sun is high, casting little shadow. After several takes in which he gets my feet stepping off the river onto the muddy sand, he glances toward the spillway to see that the boys have gone now. From the opposite direction, we hear a car horn and turn to see a shiny white SUV with green Border Patrol highlights. Oh shit, I say. He says, Relax. Put your socks on and let's go.

We approach the vehicle and see this uniformed woman sitting inside tapping out some tune with her hand on her side-view mirror. She's middle-aged and tanned as can be, her blond hair pulled back in a tight ponytail. She puts on a bright smile. What y'all doin' out here? she says.

We're shooting footage for a theater project on immigration, I say.

Oh yeah? Well, you fellas take care. You don't know the things that go on around these parts.

Yes, ma'am, the camera guy says. We're done. He starts for the car. I maintain my gaze on her bright open face, feeling the opportunity arise. Things like what? I say.

She cocks her head sideways at me. I got stories I could share, but no way am I sayin' shit on camera.

All right. Camera's off.

She looks at the invisible notes on her steering wheel, takes a sigh from deep inside her uniform and proceeds to tell us her tale.

My name's Fiona. Just Fiona for now. I come from a little town called Andrews some place east of here, and I came to El Paso with a hubby, who, well, let's just say his drinking finally closed the door on that relationship. Anyway, I got stuck here and needed work.

She tells us how she applied to the U.S. Custom Enforcement Agency and how well she did on her training, which surprised even her. How she was quickly assigned to a sector that nobody wanted because it was so bleak. She was teamed up with a more experienced partner, but soon he was sent to some other part of the river and, given how quiet it was here, they let her go solo.

I did what I wanted. I'd sit in my car and play that Reba McEntire real loud. Eat my meatball sandwiches. My signature meatball sandwiches. Anyway, one day, I'm sitting on the hood on my car when I see this kid. Must be around 8 or 9, raggedy jeans, T-shirt and tennies, just walking along the other side of the fence, grinning at me through the chain links. And in pretty good English he said, You missed them.

Missed what? I said.

And he said, I got two people across the border and you missed them. He let out a chuckle that got my dander up.

Are you sayin' you're a coyote? At your age?

I'm good too, he said. Then the little brat pulled out a wad of cash and shook it in my face. So I told him, You must have done it on somebody else's shift. You try that on mine and I'll git 'em. 6 am to 2.

Okay, deal!

And he ran off like he is gonna prove to me what a hot coyote he was. Which he did, because a few days later, he's sitting on a big rock by the fence waiting for me.

I did it.

You little liar! When?

¡Ayer! I even saw you, but you were looking the wrong way.

He told me he got a whole family of five through my sector and nobody knew it. He said that he'd been smuggling people into El Paso since he was 6 and hardly any of his clients got caught. He did a little jig and flashed the cash again.

What's your name, son?

Nacho.

Nacho what?

Not yo' business, he said with a cackle.

Very funny. You should be telling those jokes in school.

Who needs school, he said. He said he learned everything he needed from the street, English from the tourists, smuggling from watching the "experts."

These experts, are they your parents? I said. This kinda darkened his mood.

You want a piece of my sandwich?

He looked at it and nodded. I gave him half and he gobbled it up so damn quick, it got me to thinking that the money he's collecting isn't his to spend.

Fiona tells us how the next time they met, she told Nacho that she found a group of Mexican nationals in the desert, wandering around lost. She got them water and some aid before her backup came and rounded them up for deportation. Before they left, she asked them if they knew a kid named Nacho. The looks on their faces said it all.

You gotta provision them with water, Nacho, she told him. Can't be sending them into the desert like that. Nacho just nodded, like yeah, they might die.

For a while, Fiona tells us, they met every morning, traded lunches and stories about how many got across and how many caught. Until one day, I said, why don't you come over?

He looked at me and then looked past me, and said, There's a star. A big star made of lights on your montaña. It comes on every night. Está muy brillante. I always want to go up the mountain and stand right in the middle of that star.

It is pretty, I said. And I saw myself guiding him up there by the hand.

Then he got serious and he told me there's going to be a shipment of something with some mules in the next week. Watch out for them. Son peligrosos, he says.

I notify my people and they contact the DEA, and sure enough, there's a big bust just north of here in the wee hours. Somebody, not me, took the credit, but I didn't care. I just wanted to know where Nacho went. He stopped coming by our meeting spot. I worried myself sick for weeks.

Fiona puts her sunglasses on and looks toward the spillway.

Anyway, I got a report that they found a body in the river down by the Ysleta sector, and it was a boy, and though they couldn't ID it,

I knew it was him.

We tell her that we're sorry to hear it.

That boy was a pistol, she says. I know one thing. I can't hardly look at that lighted star anymore.

She revs her motor when she catches sight of those kids again, trying to scale the fence in their halfhearted way. With a threadbare smile, she nods goodbye and drives away. Maybe one of them is Nacho, the camera guys says.

Nah, I say.

OCTAVIO SOLIS is the author of more than 20 plays, including *Santos & Santos*, *El Paso Blue* and *Lydia*. Solis has won fellowships from the National Endowment of the Arts, Pew Charitable Trusts and the MacDowell Colony. In 2018, he published a memoir, *Retablos: Stories from a Life Lived Along the Border*.

WE HATE TO SEE THE SUN GO

SUNDAY, APRIL 18, 1965

From the personal diary of Lady Bird Johnson

EASTER SUNDAY, APRIL 18. Unhappily I awoke early with the sun streaming in. I had slept in the little back room because Lyndon sleeps so little these nights, and I got in several hours of work before we left by car for the little Episcopal Church in Blanco for an eleven o'clock service which sounded appealing the night before so we planned to go to St. Michaels and All Angels, Lyndon, Marvin and I. It couldn't have been a more beautiful ride in the golden sunshine over the winding road that follows the crest of the hills. We reached the little picturesque stone and redwood church just in time. Neva and I had been there the day it opened about ten years before. There was a lay Preacher and small congregation, a very simple service and then afterwards a cup of coffee in the Parish Room adjoining and shaking hands with all of the visitors and regular members. This Hill Country has turned into quite a place for people to retire to. I had worn my two piece silk dress and stiff prim sailor hat with a big bow. I felt quite satisfied for once.

After Church we found ourselves at the head of a long caravan, Lyndon driving. We passed the house that Mrs. Johnson had lived in as a young woman, in fact, spent most of her life there until she married, a comfortable looking stone house on the banks of the river. It must have been quite impressive sixty-five years ago and then we went by a nursing home to see Mr. Percy Brigham, the banker from whom Lyndon had borrowed sixty dollars to go off to San Marcos to school back in 1927 and he had helped us in all of the campaigns since. Long ago he had been Lyndon's grandfather's law partner, one of the two big men of the town. Lyndon showered him with pictures and presents, Okie quietly took some pictures of them together. In the coin of human dealings, it was time well spent.

As we left to drive home, Lyndon asked someone to quietly find out whether his mother's old home could possibly be for sale and then we drove back to Johnson City where I stopped off at the house to do a few chores and Lyndon raced ahead to A.W.'s and on by chopper to the Haywood place, accumulating along the way besides the Moursunds, Wesley and Neva and Jesse and Marianne Means. I drove to the Haywood and on my way stopped at a roadside park, bounced out of the car, went over and introduced myself to the family gathered around the picnic table and talked to them about how nice it was to have such parks along the way while Okie took a picture of us. I intend this for our Beautification Committee. Surprisingly they recognized me right off and greeted me as Mrs. Johnson. It was our last good day and we made the most of it. We spent hours out on the river, in fact, we had our lunch— sandwiches of chicken salad, which Lyndon had asked Neva to whip up on the spur of the moment. Their cook said he always had a chicken standing by and cheese and ham and everything that always tastes better out of doors, to our undoing. We talked about the short nights Lyndon had been having for several months. He asked to be waked up whenever there was an operation going out. He won't leave it alone. He said "I want to be called every time somebody dies." He can't separate himself from it. Actually, I don't want him to, no matter how painful. In Washington he seldom gets to sleep until about two, so these days down here have been balm to his soul. He talked a good deal about the job to his close friends—A.W. and Jesse and Wesley. He used the expression "when you get to be President, you have to be just." I am aware of a conscious effort on his part to change himself many times because of the job. Perhaps it is the same with everyone.

We rode around, sunned on the top deck, played bridge down below—Neva, Mariallen, Okie and I. One of the nicest moments was finding that Neva's daughter and the three grandchildren were there on the boat when I arrived. They had ridden over in the helicopter. It was a treat I had wanted to arrange for them, but it was Lyndon who just quickly bundled them up, took them along and then arranged them to get home.

I drove over to the Nicholson place and never before have I seen it so lovely. There was grass knee high with a head on it. Some of it was wild oats. Most of it was what A.W. called a sort of "love" grass, but luscious, good to eat—a paradise for cattle and none on it. We had been letting the land lie idle. We decided to move all the stock in the next morning. It was our farewell to the bluebonnets. Their whitening top showed they are getting past their peak. It was like an African safari—heading off in a Lincoln with no roads, deep in grass through fields, climbing steep banks, fording streams. A.W. said with a deep contented sigh of a born rancher, "there ain't nothing the matter with this land that a good rain won't cure." And speaking of how to get the work done around the place, he used his earthy expression. "There is no fertilizer for a man's ranch like the footsteps of the owner." More and more I begin to believe that Lyndon could be a contented retired man, but it would not always be spring and there would not always be rain.

We hate to see the sun go, but when dark fell we went to the Haywood Ranch and Marie and Marvin joined us and we had a wonderful enormous dinner on the patio, a big roast, chicken pie, fried chicken, something like "all-day-singing-and-dinner-on-the-ground" with everybody bringing covered dishes, Neva and the Moursunds and us and then we left by chopper, dropping off the Moursunds and the Wests at their ranch and then home for the end of our holiday at the LBJ Ranch with a feeling of deep contentment and farewell.

Audio diary and annotated transcript, Lady Bird Johnson, 4/18/1965 [Sunday], Lady Bird Johnson's White House Diary Collection, LBJ Presidential Library

INDEX

INDEX

6th Street
  Antique Mall, 30
Adolphus Hotel, 12
Albert Icehouse, 16
Aldrete, James, 111
Alpine, 8, 17, 32
Amarillo, 11, 30
The Amon Carter
  Museum, 86
Antelope Horns, 38
Antone, Clifford, 40
Aransas Bay, 9, 67
Arber & Sons
  Editions, 86
Armadillo World
  Headquarters, 40
Art League
  Houston, 85
Art Museum of
  South Texas, 21
Astrodome,
  10, 15, 54
Austin City Limits,
  40
Austin, 8, 25, 69, 80
Austin, Stephen F,
  10, 50
Badu, Erykah, 40
Ballroom Marfa, 86
Banita Creek
  Hall, 15
Barbecue, 9, 10, 16,
  26, 28, 67, 69, 77,
  78, 80, 88, 112
Barton Springs, 25
Baseball, 32, 42
Beaumont, 49

Benito's, 28
Bevo, 46
Big Bend National
  Park, 17, 72
The Big Easy Social
  & Pleasure
  Club, 77
The Big Texan
  Steak Steak
  Ranch, 54
Birdwatching, 22, 89
Bishop Arts
  District, 27
Black Gold, 49
Blackfoot Daisy, 38
Blake, Teal, 84
Blanco, 16, 36, 70
Blanton Museum
  of Art, 25
Blind Lemon
  Jefferson
  Memorial
  Cemetery, 93
Bluebonnets, 38
The Blue Door, 31
Books, 11, 27, 32
Brazos Bend
  State Park, 9
Brazos River, 26, 55
Bridges, Leon, 81
Briscoe, Dolph, 46
Brite Building, 73
Brownsville,
  16, 22, 88
Buc-ee's, 54
The Bucket, 17
Burrough, Bryan, 43

Bush, George W., 46
Cactus Theatre, 17
Caddo Lake
  State Park, 13
Cadillac Ranch,
  10, 30
Campbell, Earl, 37
Carr Mansion, 66
Carol Hicks Bolton
  Antiquities, 70
Carpenter Hotel, 12
Charreada, 68
Charro Days
  Fiesta, 16
Cheerleaders, 37
Cheney, Dick, 46
Chicken-Fried
  Steak, 9
Chihuahan Desert,
  33, 86, 90
The Chinati
  Foundation, 8, 87
Cisco's, 25
Ciudad Juárez,
  82, 99, 116
Cleveland,
  Thaddeus, 107
Climate, 8
Coffee, 20-33
Comal Springs, 9
Conjunto,
  68, 80, 132
Cooper's
  Bar-B-Que, 16
Corpus Christi,
  12, 16, 21, 53, 56,
  129, 130

Craighead
Green Gallery, 27
Crawfish &
Noodles, 108
Crawfish 65, 92, 108
Cycling, 8, 13, 22,
23, 24, 29, 90
*Dallas Morning
News*, 44
Dallas, 8, 10, 12,
15, 27, 37, 40, 56,
58-59, 72, 129
Dance Halls, 36, 53,
68, 70, 76, 78, 79, 81
Davis Mountains, 9
De Narvaez,
Cynta, 96
de Vaca, Cabeza, 58
Devils River, 91
Dickerson, Eric, 37
Dive Bars, 21, 25,
69, 73, 80, 90
Dixie Chicks,
11, 40, 105
DJ Screw, 11, 52
Dobie, J. Frank
60-61
Dr Pepper, 26, 47
El Paso Museum
of Art, 33
El Paso, 33, 52, 90,
99, 116
Elemi, 33
Ellerbe Fine
foods, 28
Estero Llano
Grande State
Park, 91
Executive Surf
Club, 16

Explore Ranches, 12
Fastballs, 42
Film, 11, 102
Fizz, 47
Florida's Kitchen, 15
Football, 11, 15, 16,
17, 24, 98
Fort Davis, 9, 12, 17
Fort Griffin
Fandangle, 17
Fort Worth, 28, 84
Forty Five Ten, 72
Fredericksburg,
24, 70
Freedom, 42
Friday Night
Lights, 15, 37, 98
Frio River Cabins, 12
Front Street Books,
32
Gage Hotel, 12, 73
Galveston, 38,
54, 66
Garrison
Brothers, 70
GDT Studios, 28
Geography, 9
Girls Tyme, 40
Goose Island
State Park, 13
Graves, John, 59
Guadalupe Moun-
tains National
Park, 13
Guerrero, Rosa, 99
Guns, 10, 14
Hall Arts Hotel, 27
Harrigan, Stephen,
128
Harrison House, 29

Hibiscus Café, 29
Hiram-Butler
Gallery, 83
Hoffbrau Steak &
Grill House, 30
Holland Hotel, 32
Horseback Riding,
8, 72
Hotel Emma,
12, 23
Hotel Ritual, 12, 93
Hotel Saint
Cecilia, 12
Hotter'N Hell
Hundred, 29
Houston Farmer's
Market, 65
Houston, 20, 65, 77,
83, 108
Hueco Tanks, 33
Hugo's, 65
Immigration, 14
Indian Lodge, 12
Indian
Paintrbrush, 38
Inks Lake
State Park, 13
Inn at Fulton
Harbor, 67
Jacksonville, 12, 15, 93
Jenschke Orchards,
72
Jimmy's Food
Store, 27
Johnson City,
70, 143
Johnson Space
Center, 20
Johnson, Lady
Bird, 39, 50, 143

Johnson, Lyndon B, 10, 11, 39, 50, 143

Joplin, Janis, 40

Jordan, Barbara, 36

The Joule, 27

Judd, Donald, 87

Juiceland, 69

Juneteenth, 42

Kata Robata, 65

Kay, Mary, 55

Kayaking, 25, 26

Kennedy, John F. 10, 44

Ketchup, 47

The Kimbell Art Museum, 28, 86

King Ranch, 54

King's Inn, 16

Knowles, Beyoncé, 10, 20, 40, 100

Knowles, Solange, 80

Kolaches, 9

L&J Cafe, 17, 33

Lady Bird Lake, 25

Lakewood Church, 54

Lavender Fest, 16

Live Music, 15

Lockhart, 8, 9, 100

Lone Star Cowboy Poetry Gathering, 32

Lonesome Dove, 11, 57, 129

Lost Maples State Natural Area, 13

Maines, Lloyd, 104

Marathon, 12, 73

Marfa, 8, 17, 73, 86

Margaritas, 21, 45, 83, 92

McAllen, 8, 89, 103

McKinney Falls State Park, 13

The McNay Art Museum, 85

Mementos, 15

The Menil Collection, 83

Michener, James, 46

Midland, 10, 31

Modern Art Museum of Fort Worth, 28

Museum of the Big Bend, 32

The Museum of Fine Arts, Houston, 85

Museum of the Southwest, 31

Musgraves, Kacey, 40

Music, 11, 40, 79, 81

Mustang Island State Park, 12

Mustang Island, 9

Nasher Sculpture Garden, 72

Neiman Marcus, 72

Nelson, Willie, 5

New Braunfels, 9, 36, 43

Nguyen, Trong, 108

Nicol, Scott L, 103

Odessa, 47

Ohms Cafe &

Bar, 30

Oil and Gas, 10, 27, 30, 31, 43, 49, 114

Opal's Table, 31

Orbison, Roy, 40

Oxbow Bakery, 94

Padre Island National Seashore, 21

Palestine, 9, 92

Palo Alto Battlefield National Historic Park, 22

Palo Duro Canyon State Park, 30, 72

Pancho and Lefty, 40

Parker, Quanah, 52

Parsons, Kimberly King, 120

Partain, Lendon, 114

Permian Basin, 3, 31, 47, 114, 129

Perot, Ross, 46

Petra & The Beast, 27

Pie, 94, 95

Pink Cadillacs, 55

Playboys, 40

Plaza Hotel, 12

Pool Burger, 71

Project Row Houses, 85

Pull Holes, 53

Quintanilla, Selena, 11, 21, 52

R.H. Wood House, 67

R.L.'s Blues Palace #2, 27

Raba Marfa, 88
Railroad Blues, 17, 32
Rain Lily, 38
Rancho Pillow, 12
Rattlesnakes, 24, 60
Recruiting, 37, 98
Reed, Cindy, 39
Richards, Ann 10, 36, 111
Rio Grande, 22, 33, 74
Roberts, Deborah, 100
Rodeo, 8, 15, 16, 17, 20, 28, 110
Rodgers, Randy, 98
Round Top, 9, 12, 71
Royal, Darrell, 50, 98
Ruby City, 85
Ryan, Nolan, 42
Sabal Palm Sanctuary, 22
San Antonio Missions, 13, 23, 132, 80
San Antonio, 23, 68, 85
Santa Ana National Wildlife Refuge, 89, 103
Scenic Drives, 15
Shepherd, Chris, 65
Shipping & Receiving, 28
The Silver Slipper, 77
Sinclair Fort Worth, 28

Smith, Anna Nicole, 46
Solis, Octavio, 134
Southold Farm + Cellar, 70
Stanton House, 90
The Statler, 27
Stockyards National Historic District, 28
Sulfur Springs Draw, 9
Swimming Holes, 15, 16, 17, 67, 69
Tacos, 22, 33, 68, 80, 88, 90
The Tap Bar and Restaurant, 33, 90
Taquerias, 71, 88
Terlingua Chili Cook-Off, 17, 39
Terlingua, 8, 17, 45, 73, 74, 90
Tex-Mex, 9, 20, 25, 33, 90
Texas Chili Parlor, 39
Texas Monthly, 46
Texas Rangers, 56
Texas Revolution, 38, 58
Texas State Fair, 8, 54
Texas State Railroad, 92
Texas Tornados, 40
Tom Lea Upper Park, 33
Tomanetz, Tootsie, 112

Troubadours, 40
Tucker, Tanya, 80
Turrell, James, 83
Tyler Rose Festival, 15
Tyler, 15, 93
Van Zandt, JT, 67
Van Zandt, Townes, 40, 67
Vaughan, Stevie Ray 52
The Vintage Round Top, 69
Viva Big Bend Music Festival, 32
Waco, 26, 52
Walden Retreats, 70
Walker, Jerry Jeff, 40
Wehmeyer, Peggy, 106
Wells, Noël, 102
Western Wear, 27, 31, 36, 53
Whataburger, 10, 47
Wichita Falls Brewing, 29
Wichita Falls, 29
Wildcatters, 43
Wildflowers, 15, 24, 38, 59, 70, 145
Wildseed Farms, 70
Willow House, 73
Winspear Opera House, 72
Witte Museum, 23
Wrong Store, 86
Young, Vince, 37
Ysleta Mission, 33
Zubiate, Carlos, 116